New Edition plus

Viewfinder

Topics

The American Dream

Humankind's Second Chance?

compiled and edited
by
Peter Freese

Ernst Klett Sprachen
Stuttgart

Viewfinder

Topics – New Edition plus

Unterrichtsmaterialien für die Sekundarstufe II

The American Dream

Humankind's Second Chance?

Herausgeber:
Prof. em. Dr. Dr. h.c. mult. Peter Freese

Autor:
Prof. em. Dr. Dr. h.c. mult. Peter Freese

Projekt-Team:
Dr. Martin Arndt, Münster
Prof. Dr. Mita Banerjee, Mainz
David Beal, M. A., Bochum
Cornelia Becker, Bremen
Dr. Peter Dines, Cert. Ed., Ludwigsburg
Prof. Dr. Hanspeter Dörfel †
Prof. Dr. Sabine Doff, Bremen
Dr. Claudia Drawe, Essen
OStR Dieter Düwel, Castrop-Rauxel
Prof. em. Dr. Dr. h.c. mult. Peter Freese, Paderborn
Dr. Carin Freywald †
Dr. Christine Gottstein-Strobl, Eichstätt
Dr. Nancy Grimm, Jena
Jennifer von der Grün, B. A., Dortmund
OStR Ulrich Imig, Wildeshausen
OStR Reimer Jansen, Oyten-Sagehorn
Dr. Michael Mitchell, M. A., Reken und Warwick
Prof. Dr. Michael Porsche, Paderborn
Dr. Peter-J. Rekowski, Kirchhain
StD i.K. Peter Ringeisen, M. A., Amberg
StD Karl Sassenberg, Münster
StD Dr. Annegret Schrick, Essen
OStR Ekkehard Sprenger, Kiel
StR Susanne Stadler, Wiesbaden
OStD Dr. Dietrich Theißen †
Prof. Dr. Laurenz Volkmann, Jena
Philip Wade, M. A., Cert. Ed., Amberg

1. Auflage 1 8 7 6 | 2022 21 20 19

Erstausgabe erschienen 2011 bei der Langenscheidt KG, München
Internetadresse: www.klett-sprachen.de

Verlagsredaktion: Dr. Beatrix Finke
Visuelles Konzept: Barbara Slowik, Atelier S., München
Layout: kaltner verlagsmedien GmbH, Bobingen
Druck und Bindung: Elanders GmbH, 71332 Waiblingen
Printed in Germany

ISBN 978-3-12-606909-0

9 783126 069090

Contents

*Titles provided by the editor

The American Dream

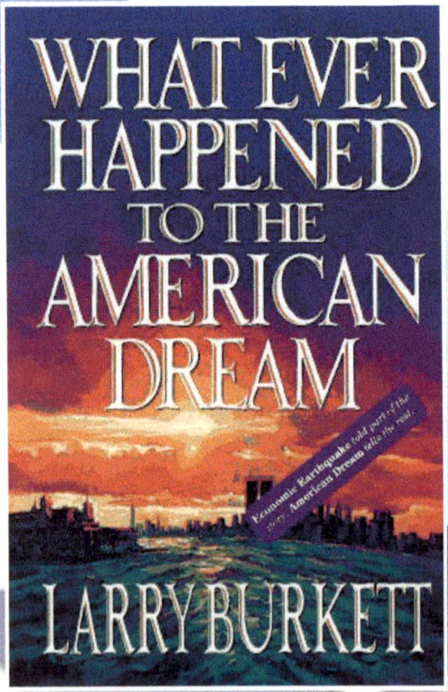

In 1931, the American historian James Truslow Adams coined the phrase "the American Dream" to describe the complex beliefs, religious promises, and political and social expectations of his nation.

This enduring notion which, in 2001, Dan Rather praised as "one of the most powerful ideas in the history of human achievement" and which, two years later, Jim Cullen described as "an idea that shaped a nation," came into being when the religious, political, and social expectations of European immigrants met with the actual realities of the New World and when the concept of 'America' took on mythic proportions for the millions of immigrants flocking there: a new promised land, a land flowing with milk and honey, an El Dorado where the Fountain of Youth bubbled forth in a pastoral landscape; the site of the New Jerusalem and the City upon the Hill where Christ's Second Coming would establish a new paradise on earth; and a new and ideal nation where the tyrannical restraints of the Old World would be replaced by human equality, liberty and brotherhood for all.

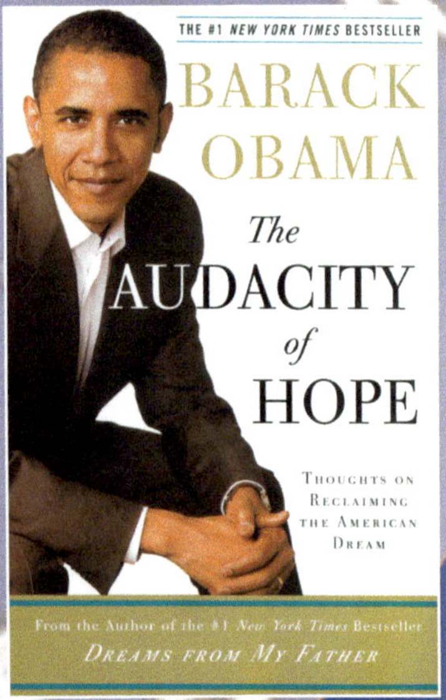

The concept has endured to this day, but as yet no one has succeeded in providing a generally acceptable definition of "the American Dream," which Adams called "the dream of a land in which life should be better and richer and fuller for every man, with opportunity for each according to his ability or achievement." However, the 'Dream' can be said to be made up of the following major elements:

- the future-oriented belief in a steady improvement of individual, communal and societal conditions of existence, that is, the belief in PROGRESS;
- the conviction that everybody can realize his or her highest ambitions by means of their own endeavors, that is, the belief in the general attainability of SUCCESS;
- the certainty that God has singled out America as his chosen country and has appointed the Americans to convert the rest of the world to true American-style democracy, that is, the belief in MANIFEST DESTINY;

- the assurance that, in the context of civilization's irresistible westward movement, ever new borderlines are to be crossed and ever new obstacles are to be surmounted, that is, the idea of the continual challenge of respective FRONTIERS;
- the belief in the American form of government of the people, by the people and for the people as the sole guarantor of LIBERTY and EQUALITY; and
- the idea that immigrants of different nationalities, different ethnic stock and different religious affiliations can be fused into a new nation, that is, the conviction expressed in the notion of the MELTING POT; or the hope that they can live peacefully together without abandoning their diverse cultures, that is, the belief in CULTURAL PLURALISM, MULTI-ETHNICITY, or MULTICULTURALISM[1].

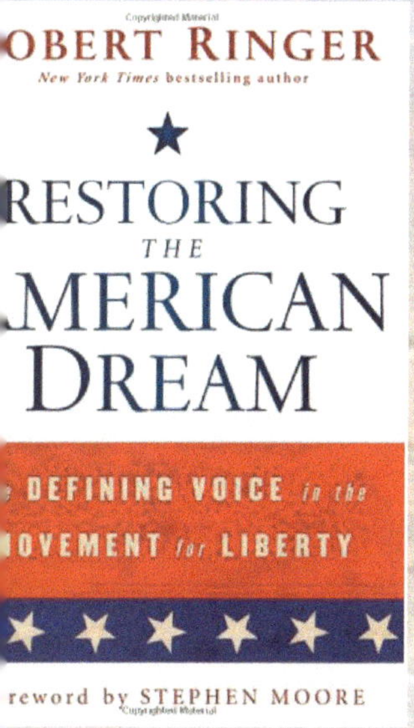

Today, the "American Dream" is a highly controversial concept. Both Hillary Clinton with her "American Dream Initiative, an opportunity agenda for the middle class and all who aspire to join it," and Barack Obama with his promise that as president he would "reclaim" the American Dream still uphold the Dream's viability. But many Americans who have lost their houses in the subprime mortgage crisis and their jobs in the ensuing financial crisis consider the 'Dream' a mendacious ideal disproved by a faulty reality and feel that it has been lost for good. Thus, Dan Rather's praise of the 'Dream' as an enduring influence which has "made us a nation of idealists, pointing us toward tomorrow and teaching us to struggle toward social justice" stands in stark contrast to Michael Moore's ironic comment: "Remember the American Dream? For those of you too young to have experienced it, this is what it used to be: If you work hard, and your company prospers, you, too, shall prosper. That dream has gone up in smoke. It has been turned into the American Bad Dream."

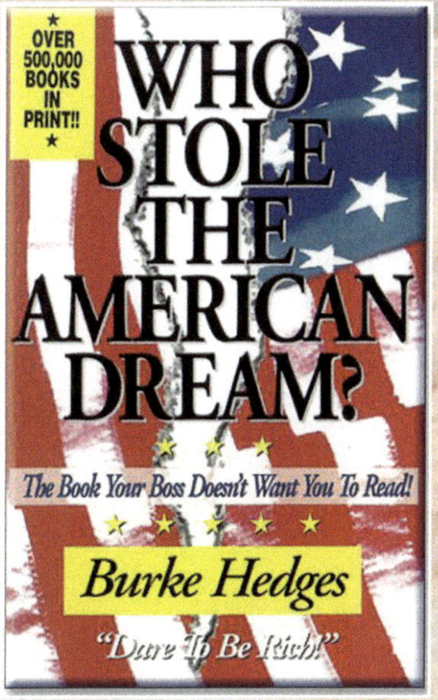

1 Dealt with in detail in the VIEWFINDER topic: Peter Freese, ed., *From Melting Pot to Multiculturalism: 'E pluribus unum'?* new rev. ed., 2005 ff.

"Dream" vs. Reality

These two German cartoons appeared around 1838 in the Neu-Ruppiner Bilderbogen *by Oehmigke and Riemschneider and are taken from Hermann von Freden and Georg Smolka, eds.,* Auswanderer: Bilder und Skizzen aus der Geschichte der deutschen Auswanderung *(Leipzig: Bibliographisches Institut AG, 1937), between pp. 32 and 33.*

New York, Wall Street 2009

The American Dream

Humankind's Second Chance?

"The admiral says that the sacred theologians and wise philosophers have well said that the earthly paradise is in the end of the east, because it is a very temperate place, so those lands which he has now discovered are, he says, 'the end of the east.'"
Journal of the First Voyage of Columbus

Edward Hicks (1780-1849), Peaceable Kingdom, *ca. 1830. This is one of more than fifty versions in which the Quaker preacher illustrated his most beloved Biblical text from Isaiah 11:6: "The wolf also shall dwell with the lamb, and the leopard shall lie down with the kid; and the calf and the young lion and the fatling together; and a little child shall lead them." In this painting, as elsewhere, Hicks also included a background scene which he thought illustrated the Biblical text, namely, William Penn making a treaty with the Native Americans.*

Edward Hicks was born in 1780 in Attleboro, now Langhorne, in Bucks County, Pennsylvania, and was well known among his fellow Quakers as a dedicated preacher whose spontaneous sermons bore the power of deep conviction and as someone who could decorate coaches and furniture and paint beautiful signs. He came to art late in life and with great reluctance, since he feared that art might be contrary to religion, but he reasoned that 'moral' paintings could provide life with additional meaning. Hicks painted 'naive' depictions of the farms and landscape of Pennsylvania, and between the mid-1820s and his death in 1849 he painted over fifty variations of his favorite theme from Isaiah 11:6. In these 'primitive' pictures he attempted to visualize the Biblical promise of a Peaceable Kingdom on earth and often linked the assurance that one day "the leopard shall lie down with the kid" with the signing of the treaty between his hero William Penn and the Native Americans of Pennsylvania, an event which he understood as a fulfilment of the prophet's promise of justice and gentleness between all living beings. His treatment of the achievement of the Peaceable Kingdom in the New World expresses the hope for a reconciliation between God and nature and between human beings, and his pictures might well be understood as early expressions of one man's 'American Dream.'

Vocabulary

temperate (adj.): (of parts of the world, climate, etc.) free from very high or very low temperatures - **peaceable** (adj.): disliking argument or quarrelling; calm and free from disorder or fighting - **kid** (n.): a young goat - **fatling** (n.): a young animal fattened for slaughter

Explanations

Quaker: The religious body called the Society of Friends came into being in England under the leadership of George Fox (1624-91), who opposed church hierarchy, doctrinal excess and pomp and called instead for a simple personal religion. His followers were called 'Quakers' either because they began to 'quake' when filled by the 'Inner Light' of the Holy Ghost or because Fox once told a judge that he should "tremble at the word of the Lord." The doctrines of the Quakers, who are against rigid creeds and think of their belief as an attitude of the mind, do not differ much from those of other denominations. Believing that the same spirit that produced the Scriptures still guides men to understand them, they have no set forms of worship and no trained leaders but assemble to await the 'Inner Light,' a direct visitation by the Holy Spirit. Since the Quakers were pacifists and declined to take oaths, they were continually persecuted until the Toleration Act of 1689. When they went to America in the 1650s, they were persecuted by the Puritans, whose theocracy they opposed. But they flourished and became widely known for their humanitarianism, which showed itself in their relations with Native Americans and in their opposition to slavery. - **William Penn:** (1644-1718), an English Quaker who, although twice imprisoned for attacking the doctrine of the Trinity and defying the Conventicle Act, continued to work for his faith in England and on the Continent. In 1681 he managed to secure the grant of Pennsylvania, and a year later he went to America to organize the colony, establish its liberal government, which was meant to guarantee fundamental civil rights, and make equitable treaties with the Native Americans. Between 1692 and 1694, Penn temporarily lost his colony, when he was accused of treason, and during these trying years he wrote *Some Fruits of Solitude* (1693), his maxims of faith and life. He visited Pennsylvania again, after it was returned to him in 1699, and in 1700 he revised its charter with the aim of making it even more democratic. In the same year he left his colony for the last time and went to England, where he was imprisoned for debt, when his deputies mismanaged the colony's affairs. In 1712, when he lost his memory, his wife took over the administration, and after her death in 1727 his sons continued his work.

Awareness

1 Collect, in class, the associations you have when hearing the term 'the American Dream,' and arrange them in the form of a mindmap. Check how many of your associations can be assigned to the six concepts which the 'Introduction' defines as the major ingredients of the Dream.

Analysis

2 Study Hicks' favorite Biblical text, Isaiah 11:6, and investigate how he translates the prophet's vision of all-embracing peace into visual imagery.

3 Compare the two "Dream vs. Reality" cartoons on p. 6 and list the differences between what the German immigrants expect to find in the New World and the 'reality' they are then confronted with. Comment on every small detail shown in the cartoons.

4 Is the Dream really over? Collect arguments for and against this position.

5 Discuss the role which, according to the cartoon above, 'money' plays for a realization of the 'American Dream.'

6 Use Columbus' journal entry as starting-point for an investigation of the '*American* Dream' as a *European* invention, that is, as a projection of unfulfilled European longings upon the New World.

Opinion

7 Discuss in how far Hicks' paintings can be understood as an illustration of important elements of the 'American Dream.'

8 What is your personal concept of the 'American Dream'? Make a list of the reasons why you would / would not want to emigrate to the U.S.

Project

9 Use the internet to collect photos, pictures, icons, slogans, etc. that use the 'Dream' concept and arrange them into a collage of the meanings the 'Dream' has in the public discourse in the U.S.

Internet Project

10 Find out what the books shown on the opening pages have to say about the 'American Dream'; www.amazon.com might be a helpful starting point.

1

James Truslow Adams

"The American Dream"*

In the midst of the Great Depression an American historian published a voluminous study, in which he dealt with what he called "the American dream." He thus coined a term which has since become the widely used and hotly contested catchphrase for the basic lure and promise of America. Since nobody has yet been able to come up with a generally accepted definition of "the American dream," it seems only logical that any consideration of this charged concept should begin with Adams' text. – James Truslow Adams, *The Epic of America* (New York: Blue Ribbon Books, 1931), pp. 404, 405, 411, 412, and 416.

Margaret Bourke-White, "Bread-Line during the Louisville Flood, Kentucky"

If [...] the things already listed were all we had had to contribute, America would have made no distinctive and unique gift to mankind. But there has been also the *American dream*, the dream of a land in which life should be better and richer and fuller for every man, with opportunity for each according to his ability or achievement. It is a difficult dream for the European upper classes to interpret adequately, and too many of us ourselves have grown weary and mistrustful of it. It is not a dream of motor cars and high wages merely, but a dream of a social order in which each man and each woman shall be able to attain to the fullest stature of which they are innately capable, and be recognized by others for what they are, regardless of the fortuitous circumstances of birth or position.

[...]

No, the American dream that has lured tens of millions of all nations to our shores in the past century has not been a dream of merely material plenty, though that has doubtless counted heavily. It has been much more than that. It has been a dream of being able to grow to fullest development as man and woman, unhampered by the barriers which had slowly been erected in older civilizations, unrepressed by social orders which had developed for the benefit of classes rather than for the simple human being of any and every class. And that dream has been realized more fully in actual life here than anywhere else, though very imperfectly even among ourselves.

[...]

The point is that if we are to have a rich and full life in which all are to share and play their parts, if the American dream is to be a reality, our communal spiritual and intellectual life must be distinctly higher than elsewhere, where classes and groups have their separate interests, habits, markets, arts, and lives. If the dream is not to prove possible of fulfillment, we might as well become stark realists, become once more class-conscious, and struggle as individuals or classes against one another. If it is to come true, those on top, financially, intellectually, or otherwise, have got to devote themselves to the "Great Society," and those who are below in the scale have got to strive to rise, not merely economically, but culturally. We cannot become a great democracy by giving ourselves up as individuals to selfishness, physical comfort, and cheap amusement. The very foundation of the American dream of a better and richer life for all is that all, in varying degrees, shall be capable of wanting to share in it. It can never be wrought into a reality by cheap people or by "keeping up with the Joneses." There is nothing whatever in a fortune merely in itself or in a man merely in himself. It all depends on what is made of each.

[...]

If we are to make the dream come true we must all work together, no longer to build bigger, but to build better. [...] In a country as big as America it is as impossible to prophesy as it is to generalize, without being tripped up, but it seems to me that there is room for hope as well as mistrust. The epic loses all its glory without the dream. The statistics of size, population, and wealth would mean nothing to me unless I could still believe in the dream.

[...]

We have a long and arduous road to travel if we are to realize our American dream in the life of our nation, but if we fail, there is nothing left but the old eternal round. The alternative is the failure of self-government, the failure of the common man to rise to full stature, the failure of all that the American dream has held of hope and promise for mankind.

Vocabulary

Intro/1 voluminous (adj.): producing or containing much writing - **Intro/2 to coin a term** (v.): to invent (a word or phrase) - **Intro/3 catchphrase** (n.): a phrase, often with little meaning, which becomes popular for a time so that everyone uses it - **Intro/3 lure** (n.): s.th. that attracts by promising pleasure - **9 weary** (adj.): /'wɪəri/ very tired - **9 mistrustful** (adj.): having or showing lack of trust - **12 to attain** (v.): to succeed in arriving at, esp. after an effort - **12 stature** (n.): /'stætʃə(r)/ the quality or position gained by development or proved worth - **13 innate** (adj.): (of qualities) which s.o. was born with - **14 fortuitous** (adj.): /fɔː(r)'tjuːɪtəs/ happening by chance, accidental; fortunate, lucky - **22 unhampered** (adj.): without difficulty in movement or activity - **23 to erect** (v.): to build or establish (a solid thing which was not there before) - **38 stark** (adj.): hard, bare, or severe in appearance; pure, complete - **41 to devote** (v.): to set apart for; to give wholly or completely to - **43 scale** (n.): a set of numbers or standards for measuring or comparing - **43 to strive** (v.): to struggle hard; to make a great effort, esp. to gain s.th. - **49 wrought**: old past tense and past part. of to work - **50 to keep up with the Joneses**: (derog.) to compete with one's neighbors socially, esp. by buying the same expensive new things that they buy - **59 to trip up** (v.): to (cause to) make a mistake as in a statement or behavior - **65 arduous** (adj.): needing much effort - **67 the old eternal round:** the accustomed procedure that repeats itself for ever

James Truslow Adams (1878-1949) was educated at Brooklyn Polytechnic Institute and Yale and spent thirteen years in business in New York before he devoted himself full-time to historical research. In 1921 he won a Pulitzer Prize for *The Founding of New England*, the first volume of a trilogy which reinterprets the ideals and achievements of the Puritans and their descendants and which was followed by *Revolutionary New England* (1923) and *New England in the Republic* (1926). Adams' other books include Provincial Society, 1690-1763 (1927), *The March of Democracy* (1932/33), *The American: The Making of a New Man* (1943), *Frontiers of American Culture* (1944), and *Big Business in a Democracy* (1945).

Explanations

Intro/1 Great Depression: The stock-market crash of 1929 set off an economic crisis, which was unprecedented with regard to its length and the poverty and tragedy it inflicted upon American society. At its depth in 1933, about one third of the labor force was without employment. Although the economic, agricultural and relief policies of President Franklin Delano Roosevelt's New Deal administration did a great deal to mitigate the effects of the depression, it was not until the government began to spend heavily for defense in the early 1940s that complete business recovery and the end of unemployment were reached.

Awareness

1 Think about, and verbalize, the contradictions expressed by the illustration on p. 10.

Comprehension

2 What does Adams warn against when he stresses that the 'Dream' is "not a dream of motor cars and high wages merely" (l. 10)?

3 What, according to Adams, must be done and what must be avoided in order to make the 'Dream' a "reality" (l. 33)? Make two lists.

4 What are the major elements of the 'American Dream' as described by Adams?

Analysis

5 Analyze the implications of Adams' vision of a "better and richer and fuller [life] for every man, with opportunity for each according to his ability or achievement" (ll. 5 ff.).

6 Collect and systematize the arguments which Adams offers in order to show that the 'Dream' is more than just the promise of material success.

Opinion

7 Is America today closer to the attainment of the 'Dream' than it was in 1931, or has the 'Dream' been lost or even turned into a 'Nightmare'? Use texts 16 to 19 to help you to substantiate your answer.

Internet Project

8 Collect information about the famous photograph by Margaret Bourke-White and the situation it shows. Use www.photo-seminars.com/Fame/MargaretWhite.htm to start with.

2 The 'American Dream' in Political Rhetoric

Since James Truslow Adams, the notion of the 'American Dream' has come to stand for a complex combination of enduring beliefs and convictions, which cannot be precisely defined. But despite its changes with time the Dream has endured, and if one looks at selected instances of political rhetoric, it becomes obvious how easily its fundamental values and promises can be made to fit the respective requirements of a given historical situation.

***Richard Milhous Nixon**, First Inaugural Address, 20 January 1969*

In pursuing our goals of full employment, better housing, excellence in education; in rebuilding our cities and improving our rural areas; in protecting our environment and enhancing the quality of life – in all these and more, we will and must press urgently forward. [...] We shall plan now for the day when our wealth can be transferred from the destruction of war abroad to the urgent needs of our people at home. The American Dream does not come to those who fall asleep. [...] As we measure what can be done, we shall promise only what we know we can produce, but as we chart our goals we shall be lifted by our dreams.

***Second Inaugural Address,** 20 January 1973*

Above all else, the time has come for us to renew our faith in ourselves and in America. In recent years, that faith has been challenged. Our children have been taught to be ashamed of their country, ashamed of their parents, ashamed of America's record at home and of its role in the world. [...] As I stand in this place, so hallowed by history, I think of others who have stood here before me. I think of the dreams they had for America, and I think of how each recognized that he needed help far beyond himself in order to make those dreams come true.

***Jimmy Carter**, Inaugural Address, 20 January 1977*

Two centuries ago our nation's birth was a milestone in the long quest for freedom, but the bold and brilliant dream which excited the founders of this nation still awaits its consummation. I have no new dream to set forth today, but rather urge a fresh faith in the old dream. [...] The American Dream endures. We must once again have full faith in our country – and in one another. I believe America can be better. We can be even stronger than before. [...] These are not just my goals. And they will not be my accomplishments, but the affirmation of our nation's continuing moral strength and our belief in an undiminished, ever-expanding American Dream.

***Ronald Reagan**, First Inaugural Address, 20 January 1981*

If we look to the answer as to why for so many years we achieved so much, prospered as no other people on Earth, it was because here in this land we unleashed the energy and individual genius of man to a greater extent than has ever been done before. [...] It is time for us to realize that we're too great a nation to limit ourselves to small dreams. We're not, as some would have us believe, doomed to an inevitable decline. I do not believe in a fate that will fall on us no matter what we do. I do believe in a fate that will fall on us if we do nothing. So, with all the creative energy at our command, let us begin an era of national renewal. Let us renew our determination, our courage, and our strength. And let us renew our faith and our hope. We have every right to dream heroic dreams. Your dreams, your hopes, your goals are going to be the dreams, the hopes, and the goals of this administration, so help me God.

***Jesse Jackson**, at the Democratic National Convention in San Francisco, 17 July 1984*

I just want young America to do me one favor. Exercise the right to dream. You must face reality – that which is. But then dream of the reality that ought to be, that must be. Live beyond the pain of reality with the dream of a bright tomorrow. Use hope and imagination as weapons of survival and progress. [...] Young America, dream.

***Geraldine Ferraro**, Nomination Acceptance Speech at the Democratic National Convention in San Francisco, 19 July 1984*

I stand before you to proclaim tonight: America is the land where dreams can come true for all of us. [...] I recall the words of Dr. Martin Luther King, Jr., who made America stronger by making America more free. He said, "Occasionally in life there are moments which cannot be completely explained by words. Their meaning can only be articulated by the inaudible language of the heart." Tonight is such a moment for me. [...] Tonight, the daughter of an immigrant from Italy has been chosen to run for Vice President in the new land my father came to love. Our faith that we can shape a better future is what the American Dream is all about. The promise of our country is that the rules are fair. If you work hard and play by the rules, you can earn your share of America's blessings. Those are the beliefs I learned from my parents. And those are the values I taught my students as a teacher in the public schools of New York City. By choosing a woman to run for the nation's second highest office, you send a powerful signal to all Americans: There are no doors we cannot unlock. We will place no limits on achievement. If we can do this, we can do anything. Tonight, we reclaim our dream. We are going to make the rules of American life work fairly for all Americans again.

***Ronald Reagan**, Second Inaugural Address, 21 January 1985*

But we, the present-day Americans, are not given to looking backward. In this blessed land, there is always a better tomorrow. [...] We believed then and now there are no limits to growth and human progress when men and women are free to follow their dreams. And we were right to believe that. [...] My fellow citizens, our Nation is poised for greatness. [...] Freedom and incentives unleash the drive and entrepreneurial genius that are the core of human progress. [...] Let us resolve that we the people will build an American opportunity society in which all of us – white and black, rich and poor, young and old – will go forward together, arm in arm. Again, let us remember that though our heritage is one of blood lines from every corner of the Earth, we are all Americans pledged to carry on this last, best hope of man on Earth. [...] It is the American sound. It is hopeful, big-hearted, idealistic, daring, decent, and fair. That's our heritage, that's our song. [We are] one people under God, dedicated to the dream of freedom that He has placed in the human heart, called upon now to pass that dream on to a waiting and hopeful world.

***Michael S. Dukakis**, Nomination Acceptance Speech at the Democratic National Convention in Atlanta, 21 July 1988*

We're going to win because we are the party that believes in the American Dream. A dream so powerful that no distance of ground, no expanse of ocean, no barrier of language, no distinction of race or creed or color can weaken its hold on the human heart. And I know, because my friends, I'm a product of that dream and I'm proud of it. A dream that brought my father to this country 76 years ago, that brought my mother and her family here one year later – poor, unable to speak English but with a burning desire to succeed in their new land of opportunity. And tonight in the presence of that marvelous woman who is my mother and who came here 75 years ago; with the memory in my heart of the young man who arrived at Ellis Island with only $25 in his pocket, but with a deep and abiding faith in the promise of America – [...] My friends, the dream that carried me to this platform is alive tonight in every part of the country – and it's what the Democratic Party is all about. [...] to every American, you are a full shareholder in our dream. And my friends, if anyone tells you that the American Dream belongs to the privileged few and not to all of us, you tell them that the Reagan era is over and that a new era is about to begin. [...] It's time to meet the challenge of the next American frontier – the challenge of building an economic future for our country that will create good jobs at good wages for every citizen in this land [...] we believe that there are no limits to what America can do. [...] But my friends, maintaining the status quo – running in place – standing still – isn't good enough for America. Opportunity for some isn't good enough for America. Because working together, we're going to forge a new era of greatness for America. [...] My friends, the dream that began in Philadelphia 200 years ago; the spirit that survived that terrible winter at Valley Forge and triumphed on the beaches at Normandy; the courage that looked Khrushchev in the eye during the Cuban missile crisis – is as strong and as vibrant today as it has ever been. [...] A new era of greatness for America. And when we leave here tonight, we will leave to build that future together. To build the future so that when our children and our grand-children look back in their time on what we did in our time; they will say that we had the wisdom to carry on the dreams of those who came before us; the courage to make our own dreams come true; and the foresight to blaze a trail for generations yet to come.

George H. W. Bush, *Inaugural Address, 20 January 1989*

America today is a proud, free nation, decent and civil, a place we cannot help but love. We know in our hearts, not loudly and proudly, but as a simple fact, that this country has meaning beyond what we see, and that our strength is a force for good. But have we changed as a nation even in our time? Are we enthralled with material things, less appreciative of the nobility of work and sacrifice? [...] No President, no government, can teach us to remember what is best in what we are. [...] America is never wholly herself unless she is engaged in high moral principle. We as a people have such a purpose today. It is to make kinder the face of the nation and gentler the face of the world. My friends, we have work to do.

William Jefferson Clinton, *First Inaugural Address, 20 January 1993*

Today, we do more than celebrate America; we rededicate ourselves to the very idea of America. An idea born in revolution and renewed through two centuries of challenge. An idea tempered by the knowledge that, but for fate, we – the fortunate and the unfortunate – might have been each other. An idea ennobled by the faith that our nation can summon from its myriad diversity the deepest measure of unity. An idea infused with the conviction that America's long heroic journey must go forever upward.

Statement to the Democratic Leadership Council, *1993*

The American Dream that we were all raised on is a simple but powerful one – if you work hard and play by the rules you should be given a chance to go as far as your God-given ability will take you.

Second Inaugural Address, *20 January 1997*

The promise of America was born in the 18th century out of the bold conviction that we are all created equal. It was extended and preserved in the 19th century, when our nation spread across the continent, saved the union, and abolished the awful scourge of slavery. Then, in turmoil and triumph, that promise exploded onto the world stage to make this the American Century. [...] We – the American people – we are the solution. Our founders understood that well and gave us a democracy strong enough to endure for centuries, flexible enough to face our common challenges and advance our common dreams in each new day. [...] Thirty-four years ago, the man whose life we celebrate today spoke to us down there, at the other end of this Mall, in words that moved the conscience of a nation. Like a prophet of old, he told of his dream that one day America would rise up and treat all its citizens as equals before the law and in the heart. Martin Luther King's dream was the American Dream. His quest is our quest: the ceaseless striving to live out our true creed. Our history has been built on such dreams and labors. And by our dreams and labors we will redeem the promise of America in the 21st century. [...] Yes, let us build our bridge. A bridge wide enough and strong enough for every American to cross over to a blessed land of new promise. May those generations whose faces we cannot yet see, whose names we may never know, say of us here that we led our beloved land into a new century with the American Dream alive for all her children; with the American promise of a more perfect union a reality for all her people; with America's bright flame of freedom spreading throughout all the world.

***George W. Bush,** First Inaugural Address, 20 January 2001*

It is the American story; a story of flawed and fallible people, united across the generations by grand and enduring ideals. The grandest of these ideals is an unfolding American promise: that everyone belongs, that everyone deserves a chance, that no insignificant person was ever born. Americans are called to enact this promise in our lives and in our laws. And though our nation has sometimes halted, and sometimes delayed, we must follow no other course. [...] Much time has passed since Jefferson arrived for his inaugural. The years and changes accumulate. But the themes of this day he would know: our nation's grand story of courage, and its simple dream of dignity.

***Second Inaugural Address,** 20 January 2005*

America's vital interests and our deepest beliefs are now one. From the day of our Founding, we have proclaimed that every man and woman on this earth has rights, and dignity, and matchless value, because they bear the image of the Maker of Heaven and earth. Across the generations we have proclaimed the imperative of self-government, because no one is fit to be a master, and no one deserves to be a slave. Advancing these ideals is the mission that created our Nation. [...] In America's ideal of freedom, citizens find the dignity and security of economic independence, instead of laboring on the edge of subsistence. This is the broader definition of liberty that motivated the Homestead Act, the Social Security Act, and the G.I. Bill of Rights. And now we will extend this vision by reforming great institutions to serve the needs of our time. To give every American a stake in the promise and future of our country, we will bring the highest standards to our schools, and build an ownership society. We will widen the ownership of homes and businesses, retirement savings and health insurance – preparing our people for the challenges of life in a free society. By making every citizen an agent of his or her own destiny, we will give our fellow Americans greater freedom from want and fear, and make our society more prosperous and just and equal. [...] When the Declaration of Independence was first read in public and the Liberty Bell was sounded in celebration, a witness said, "It rang as if it meant something." In our time it means something still. America, in this young century, proclaims liberty throughout all the world, and to all the inhabitants thereof. Renewed in our strength – tested, but not weary – we are ready for the greatest achievements in the history of freedom.

***Senator Hillary Rodham Clinton,** with Senator Tom Carper, and Governor Tom Vilsack, "Saving the American Dream," Blueprint Magazine, 22 July 2006*

For 230 years, Americans have been united by a simple, common dream that tomorrow will be better than today. The promise of American life, handed on through a dozen generations, rests on this basic bargain: All of us should have the opportunity to live up to our God-given potential, and the responsibility to make the most of it. In the 20th century, that basic bargain built the greatest middle class the world has ever known. The expansion of opportunity in return for hard work and sacrifice made us the richest, safest, strongest nation on earth, and enabled us to defeat fascism and communism. We ended the last century with America's economic might at its zenith, with Americans at their most optimistic, and with nearly all who endeavored to make the most of their opportunities and talents getting ahead in life. Over the last five years we've taken a different direction – one that offered the greatest help to those with the most wealth, under the mistaken belief that when the wealthy do even better, the middle class will eventually get their share. But this economic philosophy has shortchanged America and failed the middle class, too. For the first time ever, we've had four straight years of rising productivity and falling incomes. Americans are earning less, while the costs of a middle-class life have soared: In the past five years, college costs are up 50 percent, health care 73 percent, and gasoline more than 100 percent. U.S. companies and workers face new challenges because they have to compete against companies and workers from other countries that have made education the top national priority, take energy efficiency seriously, and spend half as much on health care as we do. These trends aren't just a burden for middle-class families. They undermine our way of life, because middle-class strength and growth have been the backbone of America. Together we can face that challenge. Throughout our history, America has responded to new challenges with a new faith in our basic bargain. The world has changed over the past 50 years, and the terms of our basic bargain must keep pace. The chance for every American to get ahead, regardless of background, is the engine of America's economic growth and social progress. A growing economy and a growing middle class go hand in hand. To remain strong in the world, the American Dream must be strong and alive here at home. And as we continue to navigate through these changing economic times, restoring the promise of the American Dream is the central economic issue of our time. That's why the three of us have spent the past year developing the American Dream Initiative, an opportunity agenda for the middle class and all who aspire to join it. [...] We will offer a new opportunity agenda that secures the pillars of the American Dream:

Every American should have the opportunity and responsibility to go to college and earn a degree, and to get the lifelong training they need. Every worker should have the opportunity and responsibility to save for a secure retirement. Every business should have the opportunity to grow and prosper in the strongest private economy on Earth, and the responsibility to equip workers with the same tools of success as management. Every individual should have the opportunity and responsibility to start building wealth from day one, and the security and community that come from owning a home. Every family should have the opportunity to afford health insurance for their children, and the responsibility to obtain it.

Of all the aspirations that make up the American Dream, perhaps the most important is the opportunity to go to college. College is the key to whether America will get ahead in a competitive world, and whether we can expand and strengthen the middle class here at home. We propose a plan to produce one million more college graduates a year by 2015 – so that within a decade, more than half our young people will finish college with a degree. [...] The pillars of the American Dream – a college degree, a home, a secure retirement, and the chance to get ahead in a growing economy – are central to our basic values. When we demand responsibility, it makes our families, our markets, and our democracy stronger. When our success depends on how hard we work, not how well we're born, there is no limit to how high we'll reach or how far we'll go. America needs a new direction steeped in our oldest values. The struggles of the last few years are America's past, not America's future. The American Dream has just begun.

***Barack Obama,** Speech in Bettendorf, Iowa, 7 November 2007*

Americans share a faith in simple dreams. A job with wages that can support a family. Health care that we can count on and afford. A retirement that is dignified and secure. Education and opportunity for our kids. Common hopes. American dreams. [...] What is unique about America is that we want these dreams for more than ourselves – we want them for each other. That's why we call it the American Dream.

Vocabulary

Use your own dictionary.

Explanations

2 inaugural address: the formal speech given by the newly elected president at the special ceremony during which he is introduced into office – **75 National Convention**: Every four years both the Republicans and the Democrats stage national conventions, during which the candidates for the presidency and vice-presidency are nominated and the election platforms are passed. – **89 nomination acceptance speech**: the speech in which the newly chosen (vice-) presidential candidates accept the nomination and outline their strategy to their party convention – **98 Dr. Martin Luther King, Jr.**: see text 4 – **170 Ellis Island**: an island in Upper New York Bay southwest of Manhattan, which was long the site of an arsenal and a fort, but became famous when it replaced Castle Garden as the chief U.S. immigration station in 1892. Today, the island, which sometimes received as many as 15,000 immigrants in one day, is a museum. – **190 Valley Forge**: a site on the Schuylkill River, about twenty miles northwest of Philadelphia. General Washington's army wintered there in 1777/78, following the defeats at Brandywine and Germantown. The severe suffering and persistent patriotism of most of the soldiers have made the locality a national shrine. – **191 the beaches of Normandy**: Operation Overlord, the Allied Invasion of the European continent during World War II began on 6 June 1944 (D-Day) on "the beaches of Normandy." – **192 Nikita Sergeyevich Khrushchev**: (1894-1971) a communist leader who emerged from the power struggle after the death of Stalin as the first secretary of the Communist Party (1953-64) and the premier of the U.S.S.R. (1958-64) – **193 Cuban missile crisis**: a major cold war confrontation between the U.S. and the Soviet Union. After the Bay of Pigs Invasion, the U.S.S.R. increased its support of Castro's Cuban regime, and in the summer of 1962, Khrushchev secretly decided to install ballistic missiles in Cuba. When the U.S. discovered the missile launching sites, President Kennedy publicly denounced the Soviet actions on 22 October 1962, imposed a naval blockade on Cuba, and declared that any missile launched from Cuba would warrant a full-scale retaliatory attack. For a few days the threat of nuclear war cast its shadow, but on 24 October, Russian ships carrying missiles to Cuba turned back, and when Khrushchev agreed on 28 October to withdraw the missiles and dismantle the sites, the crisis ended as suddenly as it had begun. – **253 American Century**: The term was coined by Henry Luce, the publisher of *Time*, to claim the historical role of the U.S. during the 20th century. In an editorial of 17 February 1941 in *Life*, he urged the U.S. to give up isolationism, adopt a missionary's role, and enter World War II to defend democratic values. – **295 Thomas Jefferson**: (1743-1826) the principal author of the Declaration of Independence (1776) and the third President of the U.S. (1801-09). As an influential Founding Father, he made the Louisiana Purchase (1803), and arranged for the Lewis and Clark Expedition (1804-06). – **314 Homestead Act**: The original Act, signed into law by President Abraham Lincoln in 1862, gave everyone who was twenty-one or older and had never taken up arms against the U.S. government, including freed slaves, a freehold title to up to 160 acres (= 65 hectares) of undeveloped federal land west of the Mississippi. – **314 Social Security Act**: Drafted during President Roosevelt's first term and signed in 1935, this Act attempted to limit the dangers of old age, poverty, and unemployment, and provided several social welfare and social insurance programs. – **314 G. I. Bill of Rights**: The Servicemen's Readjustment Act of 1944, generally known as the G.I. Bill, provided college or vocational education as well as one year of unemployment compensation for veterans returning from World War II (referred to as G.I.s). It also provided different types of loans for returning veterans to buy homes and start businesses. – **328 Liberty Bell**: Located in Philadelphia, the Liberty Bell is is a symbol of American Independence. Cast in 1752 with the lettering "Proclaim liberty throughout all the land unto all the inhabitants thereof" (Leviticus 25:10), it cracked when first rung after its arrival in Philadelphia and was twice recast by local workmen.

The Immigrant's Dream

Awareness

1 Consider the circumstances under which convention speeches, nomination acceptance speeches and inaugural addresses are given and discuss the degree to which such speeches are believable.

Analysis

2 Explain the meaning of Nixon's assertion that "the American Dream does not come to those who fall asleep" (ll. 16f.).

3 Collect the major elements of 'The Immigrant's Dream' as conjured up by Dukakis, and relate them to the poster with that title on page 17.

4 Compare the definitions of the 'Dream' provided by Geraldine Ferraro (ll. 106f.), Bill Clinton (ll. 242ff.), and Hillary Clinton (ll. 341ff.).

5 What does Bill Clinton mean by talking about "the idea of America" (l. 230)?

6 Analyze the rhetorical means which each politician employs to make his promises of a better future convincing.

7 In what ways do some of the speakers employ references to persons and events of earlier American history in order to strengthen and enhance their claims and promises?

8 Which role does "the middle class" play in Hillary Clinton's concept of "restoring the promise of the American Dream" (ll. 389f.)?

9 How is Obama's definition of the 'Dream' related to that of Ferraro and both Clintons?

10 Connect what each speaker says about the 'Dream' to its six major ingredients as outlined in the Introduction and try to identify the common denominator which links all speeches.

Opinion

11 Consider the relation between the material and the spiritual implications of the 'Dream' as explained by George H. W. Bush in the light of the cartoon on page 16.

12 Comment on Reagan's claim that "we're too great a nation to limit ourselves to small dreams" (ll. 62f.).

13 Discuss in how far Dukakis' promise to make every American "a full shareholder in our dream" (l. 175) is a contradiction in terms.

14 Comment on Jackson's advice that young people should "use hope and imagination as weapons of survival and progress" (ll. 85ff.).

15 Comment on what George W. Bush has to say about the "unfolding American promise" (ll. 289f.).

16 In November 2008, the Swiss Ambassador to the U.S. said in *Blick*: "Für mich ist Obama die Personifizierung des American Dream, des Glaubens daran, dass alles möglich ist." Comment on that statement in the light of Obama's performance as President.

17 In 2008, *Focus Online* reported: "Jeder Mensch kann unabhängig von seiner Herkunft durch eigene Leistung und Willensstärke etwas aus seinem Leben machen – ja, zu Reichtum und hohem Ansehen kommen. Das ist die Quintessenz des 'American Dream'. Mit der Wahl Barack Hussein Obamas zum ersten schwarzen US-Präsidenten ist dieser Traum Wirklichkeit geworden." Comment.

Project

18 Form two parties which use the internet to find arguments for either Hillary Clinton' claim that "the American Dream has just begun" (l. 428) or the claim that "the American Dream Is Over" expressed on the photograph on page 6. For the latter position the website "The American Dream: Waking People Up and Getting Them to Realize that the American Dream Is Quickly Becoming the American Nightmare," http://endoftheamericandream.com/ might be useful.

19 The complete texts of all inauguration speeches from Jimmy Carter to Barack Obama with biographical notes and annotations are available on the CD-ROM in the Resource Book. Study each text, or one or some of them, in toto and relate the respective meaning of the 'Dream' to the historical situation in which each speech is delivered.

20 Listen to Carter's Inaugural Address (on the CD) and test your listening comprehension by doing the accompanying test.

21 Listen to Obama's "American Dream Speech" delivered in Bettendorf (on the CD) and discuss his notion of the 'Dream.'

3 Studs Terkel

The 'American Dream' as Seen by American Citizens

In 1980, Studs Terkel published a bestselling collection of interviews with about one hundred Americans from all realms of life. He found that "the old dream is still dreamt" and that "we've always managed, despite our worst, unbelievably nativist actions to rejuvenate ourselves, to bring in new people. Every new group comes in believing more firmly in the American Dream than the one that came a few years before." In 1988, Terkel continued his investigation of the 'Dream' in yet another collection of interviews, and this time he encountered a widespread loss of belief and a "deepening chasm between the haves – and have-somewhats – and the have-nots." Here are some of the definitions of the 'Dream' which he was offered by the people he interviewed. – Studs Terkel, *American Dreams Lost and Found* (New York: Ballantine Books, 1981), pp. 42; 96; 73; 137; 56; 316f.; 63; 178; and *The Great Divide: Second Thoughts on the American Dream* (New York: Avon Books, 1989), p. 70.

The middle-aged president of a corporation

The American Dream is to be better off than you are. How much money is 'enough money'? 'Enough money' is always a little bit more than you have.

An African American newspaper columnist from Chicago

My dreams have not expired entirely. There are moments when I waver between despair and hopelessness and flashes of inspiration. Years ago, when we were in trouble, we thought we could one day go north. Well, we are north now. We are at that Promised Land. The Promised Land has less hope now than it had when we were not in the Promised Land. We used to say: "We're being abused now, but one day we'll have the ballot. One of these days we're not gonna have presidents and governors who abuse us. One of these days the Ku Klux Klan is not gonna be around lynching us." All that has happened. But we didn't realize that there were some basic corrections that haven't yet been made.

A historian from New England

The American Dream always has a greater force when you don't already have it. People who grew up without it are told if you can only work long enough and hard enough, you can get that pot of gold at the end of the rainbow. When you already have the pot of gold, the dream loses its force. You can't aspire after anything material if, in fact, you're trying to get rid of the material things, [...] You need some alternative way of giving meaning to your life.

A twenty-five-year-old Hollywood actor

I guess I'm still looking for the American Dream. To me, it's people having control over their lives.

The Native American author Vine Deloria

You have to ask yourself: What kind of people were these that came here? They must have been absolutely frantic to set down roots. It was more than subduing the land. I mean, that's a hell of a toll to pay for the right to live on a piece of land.

Maybe the American Dream is in the past, understanding who you are instead of looking to the future: What are you going to be? 'Cause we've kind of reached the future. I'm not just talking about nostalgia. I'm talking about finding familiar guideposts.

A radio commentator from California

I worry about our young people. Do they have the dreams, the guts, the sinews, the red-blooded ability, to preserve our way of life? The thing our grandparents came over here to find. They found a nation founded, if you'll pardon the expression, under God and a Divine Constitution. Every youngster should have the dream of becoming president of the United States. Of course, I believe in Horatio Alger, and I love it.

The daughter of a Hollywood producer

The American Dream is really money.

A businesswoman from Lancashire

I think the American dream for most people today is just survival. When people came here from the old country, it was for a better life, not just survival. I see that people that come over today seem to prosper faster than the ones who were born here. Maybe it's because they know what it is to do without. They scrimp and save and live meagerly, where the American person, no matter what color, is spoiled. They're more docile, where the new people seem to stick together and help one another. But the average American is just out to help himself, to survive.

A Japanese-American from Seattle

The American Dream? I think: for whites only.

Background Reading

In Kurt Vonnegut's novel *God Bless You, Mr. Rosewater, or Pearls Before Swine* (1965), which presents a black humor variation of the Horatio Alger myth in order to debunk the American Dream of 'from rags to riches,' the narrator says:

> When the United States of America, which was meant to be a Utopia for all, was less than a century old, Noah Rosewater and a few men like him demonstrated the folly of the Founding Fathers in one respect: those sadly recent ancestors had not made it the law of the Utopia that the wealth of each citizen should be limited. [...] Thus did a handful of rapacious citizens come to control all that was worth controlling in America. Thus was the savage and stupid and entirely inappropriate and unnecessary and humorless American class system created. [...] Thus the American dream turned belly up, turned green, bobbed to the scummy surface of cupidity unlimited, filled with gas, went bang in the noonday sun.

In Tom Robbins' novel *Half Asleep in Frog Pajamas* (1994), a poor Filipina, who has worked her way up, earned her MBA, and now tries to realize her personal 'Dream' as a stockbroker, has this to say about the state of the 'Dream' in the nineties:

> The American dream is wasted upon those who never dreamed in the first place. Now that the schism between rich and poor has grown so wide, the old-style, anything-is-possible-in-America dreams are falling through the crack. Today, the road to the pot of gold is paved with lottery tickets and frivolous lawsuits. A thoroughly cheesy way to go.

Vocabulary

Intro/2 realm (n.): a world; an area - **Intro/3 nativist** (adj.): believing in nativism, that is, a policy defined by hate or fear of foreigners that favors native inhabitants as opposed to immigrants - **Intro/3 to rejuvenate** (v.): to make or become young again - **4 columnist** (n.): a person who writes a regular article for a newspaper or magazine - **5 to waver** (v.): to be uncertain or unsteady in movement or decision - **8 to abuse** (v.): to put to wrong use, use badly; to handle without care; treat badly - **8 ballot** (n.): the right to vote - **9 gonna**: coll. for 'going to' - **15 to aspire** (v.): to direct one's hopes and efforts to some great or important aim - **22 frantic** (adj.): in an uncontrolled state of feeling; wildly anxious, afraid, happy - **22 to subdue** (v.): to conquer or control the actions of - **22 toll** (n.): /təʊl/ here: the cost in health, life, etc., from illness, an accident, etc. - **28 guts** (n. pl.): (informal) bravery, determination; value, force - **28 sinews** (n.pl.): /'sɪnjuːz/ means of strength and support - **28 red-blooded** (adj.): (of a person's behavior, etc.) bold, strong - **37 to scrimp** (v.) to try to save as much money as you can even though you have very little - **38 meager** (adj.): (BrE -re) having much less than you need - **38 docile** (adj.): quiet and easily controlled - **62 stockbroker** (n.): s.o. whose job is buying and selling stocks, bonds, and shares - **64 to be wasted (up)on s.o.**: if s.th. is wasted (up)on s.o. they are too stupid or unsuitable to be able to use or enjoy it - **64 schism** (n.): /'s(k)ɪzəm/ the separation of a group into two groups - **66 crack** (n.): a very narrow space between two things or two parts of s.th. - **66 frivolous** (adj.): not serious or sensible

Explanations

7 Promised Land: (in the Bible) the land of Canaan promised by God to Abraham and his people; hence metaphorically a place or condition not yet experienced, which one hopes or believes will bring happiness or success (for many blacks from the slave-holding South the North seemed to be the 'promised land') - **9 Ku Klux Klan**: the name of two secret terrorist societies. The original Klan, organized in 1865 as an instrument against reconstructionism, was composed of local committees and intended to keep the newly freed blacks in a subservient condition. It used various methods of instilling fear, such as masks, flowing white robes, horseback parades and raids by night, whippings, and tarring and feathering. The first general organization of local Klans took place in 1867, with the election of N. B. Forrest, an ex-Confederate general, as Grand Wizard, and such other officers as Grand Dragons, Grand Titans, Goblins, Furies, and Ghouls. This fantastic use of the macabre was effective, and the Klan remained powerful in Southern politics and local affairs into the 1870s. The more recent Ku Klux Klan movement has been nation-wide, originating in Georgia in 1915, but spreading to many Northern regions. Based on a program of white supremacy, nativism, fundamentalism, anti-Semitism, and anti-Catholicism, it has had considerable political influence. - **20 Vine Deloria**: a Sioux who was born in 1933 and came to public attention with the publication of his book *Custer Died for Your Sins*: An Indian Manifesto (1969). Deloria, who writes about the situation of Native Americans in the U.S. with ironic wit and destroys the stereotypes and myths which white society has built up about the 'red man,' is one of the most prominent spokesmen for Native American nationalism. - **31 Horatio Alger**: /'ældʒə(r)/ (1834-99), an erstwhile Unitarian minister and the enormously successful author of nearly 130 popular books for boys, all based on the principle that a struggle against poverty and temptation inevitably leads a boy to wealth and fame. His most noted hero was the central figure in the Ragged Dick series, and it is estimated that more than twenty million copies of his novels were published. Consequently, his name became a byword for the American myth of success. - **61 Filipina** (n.): a female inhabitant of the Philippines - **62 MBA** (n.): Master of Business Administration; a university degree in the skills needed to be in charge of a business

Comprehension

1 What does the black newspaper columnist from Chicago imply when he says "Well, we are north now" (ll. 6f.)?
2 What does Vine Deloria mean by speculating that "maybe the American Dream is in the past" (l. 24)?
3 Describe the positions of Tom Robbins' heroine and of Kurt Vonnegut's narrator in your own words.
4 Make a list of the aspects of the 'Dream' which are criticized by the interviewees.

Analysis

5 For which reasons do certain groups of Americans think they are excluded from the 'Dream'?
6 Contrast the radio commentator's position with that of Tom Robbins' heroine and work out the differences.

Opinion

7 What do you think of the New England historian's observation that the 'Dream' is only attractive as long as it remains unfulfilled?
8 In his poem "America Was Promises," Archibald MacLeish says: "America was always promises. From the first voyage and the first ship there were promises - [...] America was promises - to whom?" Why would you (not) agree that MacLeish's question is the crucial question any discussion of the 'Dream' will finally lead to?

Projects

9 Read Dudley Randall's poem "The Melting Pot" (in the Viewfinder Topic *From Melting Pot to Multiculturalism*, p. 35) and discuss what he has to say about the chances of African Americans to achieve the 'Dream.'
10 Study (a) the cover stories in *Time* of 18 November 1991 about "California, the Endangered Dream" and in *Der Spiegel* of 6 October 2003 about "California: Das verkommene Paradies" and (b) the cover stories in *Time* of 1 November 2010 about "How to Restore the American Dream" and in *Der Spiegel* of 30 October 2010 about "Die verzweifelten Staaten von Amerika," and report on what you have learned about the state of the 'Dream.'

4

Martin Luther King, Jr.

"I Have a Dream"

When, on 28 August 1963, about 250,000 black and white people staged the March on Washington to demonstrate for a better Civil Rights legislation, Martin Luther King, Jr. delivered this famous speech in front of the Lincoln Memorial. – *Negro History Bulletin*, 31, 5 (May1968), 16f.

Five score years ago, a great American, in whose symbolic shadow we stand today, signed the Emancipation Proclamation. This momentous decree came as a great beacon of hope to millions of Negro slaves, who had been seared in the flames of withering injustice. It came as a joyous daybreak to end the long night of their captivity.

But one hundred years later, the Negro still is not free. One hundred years later, the life of the Negro is still sadly crippled by the manacle of segregation and the chains of discrimination.

One hundred years later, the Negro lives on a lonely island of poverty in the midst of a vast ocean of material prosperity. One hundred years later, the Negro is still languishing in the corners of American society and finds himself an exile in his own land. So we've come here today to dramatize a shameful condition.

In a sense we have come to our Nation's Capital to cash a check. When the architects of our great republic wrote the magnificent words of the Constitution and the Declaration of Independence, they were signing a promissory note to which every American was to fall heir. This note was a promise that all men, yes, black men as well as white men, would be guaranteed to the inalienable rights of life, liberty, and the pursuit of happiness.

It is obvious today that America has defaulted on this promissory note insofar as her citizens of color are concerned. Instead of honoring this sacred obligation, America has given the Negro people a bad check, a check that has come back marked "insufficient funds."

But we refuse to believe that the bank of justice is bankrupt. We refuse to believe that there are insufficient funds in the great vaults of opportunity of this nation. So we have come to cash this check, a check that will give us upon demand the riches of freedom and security of justice.

We have also come to this hallowed spot to remind America of the fierce urgency of Now. This is not time to engage in the luxury of cooling off or to take the tranquilizing drug of gradualism. Now is the time to make real the promise of democracy. Now is the time to rise from the dark and desolate valley of segregation to the sunlit path of racial justice. Now is the time to lift our nation from the quicksands of racial injustice to the solid rock of brotherhood. Now is the time to make justice a reality to all of God's children.

It would be fatal for the nation to overlook the urgency of the moment and to underestimate the determination of it's colored citizens. This sweltering summer of the Negro's legitimate discontent will not pass until there is an invigorating autumn of freedom and equality. 1963 is not an end but a beginning. Those who hope that the Negro needed to blow off steam and will now be content will have a rude awakening if the nation returns to business as usual.

There will be neither rest nor tranquility in America until the Negro is granted his citizenship rights. The whirlwinds of revolt will continue to shake the foundations of our nation until the bright day of justice emerges.

But there is something that I must say to my people who stand on the warm threshold which leads into the palace of justice. In the process of gaining our rightful place we must not be guilty of wrongful deeds.

Let us not seek to satisfy our thirst for freedom by drinking from the cup of bitterness and hatred. We must ever conduct our struggle on the high plane of dignity and discipline. We must not allow our creative protest to degenerate into physical violence. Again and again we must rise to the majestic heights of meeting physical force with soul force.

The marvelous new militancy which has engulfed the Negro community must not lead us to a distrust of all white people, for many of our white brothers, as evidenced by their presence here today, have come to realize that their destiny is tied up with our destiny. They have come to realize that their freedom is inextricably bound to our freedom. We cannot walk alone.

And as we walk, we must make the pledge that we shall always march ahead. We cannot turn back. There are those who are asking the devotees of civil rights, "When will you be satisfied?" We can never be satisfied as long as the Negro is the victim of the unspeakable horrors of police brutality.

We can never be satisfied as long as our bodies, heavy with the fatigue of travel, cannot gain lodging in the motels of the highways and the hotels of the cities. We cannot be satisfied as long as the Negro's basic mobility is from a smaller ghetto to a larger one.

We can never be satisfied as long as our children are stripped of their selfhood and robbed of their dignity by signs stating "for white only." We cannot be satisfied as long as a Negro in Mississippi cannot vote and a Negro in New York believes he has nothing for which to vote. No, no we are not satisfied and we will not be satisfied until justice rolls down like waters and righteousness like a mighty stream.

I am not unmindful that some of you have come here out of your trials and tribulations. Some of you have come fresh from narrow jail cells. Some of you have come from areas where your quest for freedom left you battered by storms of persecutions and staggered by the winds of police brutality. You have been the veterans of creative suffering. Continue to work with the faith that unearned suffering is redemptive.

Go back to Mississippi; go back to Alabama; go back to South Carolina; go back to Georgia; go back to Louisiana; go back to the slums and ghettos of our modern cities, knowing that somehow this situation can and will be changed. Let us not wallow in the valley of despair.

So I say to you, my friends, that even though we must face the difficulties of today and tomorrow, I still have a dream. It is a dream deeply rooted in the American dream. I have a dream that one day this nation will rise up and live out the true meaning of its creed. We hold these truths to be self-evident that all men are created equal.

I have a dream that one day on the red hills of Georgia the sons of former slaves and the sons of former slave owners will be able to sit down together at the table of brotherhood.

I have a dream that one day even the state of Mississippi, a state sweltering with the heat of oppression, will be transformed into an oasis of freedom and justice.

I have a dream that my four little children will one day live in a nation where they will not be judged by the color of their skin but by the content of their character. I have a dream today.

I have a dream that one day down in Alabama, with its vicious racists, with its governor having his lips dripping with the words of interposition and nullification; that one day right down in Alabama little black boys and black girls will be able to join hands with little white boys and white girls as sisters and brothers. I have a dream today.

I have a dream that one day every valley shall be exalted, and every hill and every mountain shall be made low, the rough places will be made plains and the crooked places will be made straight and the glory of the Lord shall be revealed and all flesh shall see it together.

This is our hope. This is the faith that I will go back to the South with.

With this faith we will be able to hew out of the mountain of despair a stone of hope. With this faith we will be able to transform the jangling discords of our nation into a beautiful symphony of brotherhood.

With this faith we will be able to work together, to pray together, to struggle together, to go to jail together, to climb up for freedom together, knowing that we will be free one day. This will be the day when all of God's children will be able to sing with new meaning "My country 'tis of thee, sweet land of liberty, of thee I sing. Land where my father's died, land of the Pilgrim's pride, from every mountainside, let freedom ring!" And if America is to be a great nation, this must become true.

So let freedom ring from the hilltops of New Hampshire.

Let freedom ring from the mighty mountains of New York.

Let freedom ring from the heightening Alleghenies of Pennsylvania.

Let freedom ring from the snow-capped Rockies of Colorado.

Let freedom ring from the curvaceous slopes of California. But not only that.

Let freedom ring from Stone Mountain of Georgia.

Let freedom ring from Lookout Mountain of Tennessee.

Let freedom ring from every hill and molehill of Mississippi and every mountainside, let freedom ring.

And when we allow freedom to ring, when we let it ring from every village and every hamlet, from every state and every city, we will be able to speed up that day when all of God's children, black men and white men, Jews and Gentiles, Protestants and Catholics, will be able to join hands and sing in the words of the old spiritual, "Free at last, free at last. Thank God Almighty, we are free at last."

Martin Luther King, Jr. (1929-68) was born in Atlanta, Georgia, and educated at Morehouse College and Crozier Theological Seminary. He was ordained a minister in 1947, and attended Boston University where he received his Ph.D. In 1954 he became minister of the Montgomery (Alabama) Dexter Avenue Baptist Church. He headed the Montgomery bus boycott of 1956, for which he was jailed and his house bombed. Out of this boycott grew the Southern Christian Leadership Conference (SCLC), which he led. In 1959, King moved to Atlanta to be co-pastor with his father of the Ebenezer Baptist Church. In 1960, when the sit-in movement began, the SCLC was quick to support it and to help form the Student Non-Violent Coordinating Committee (SNCC). King himself joined the Atlanta sit-ins in the fall of 1960. He was arrested, jailed, and denied bail, but presidential candidate John F. Kennedy intervened and had King freed. In the 1960s King led various campaigns and protest marches, such as the demonstrations in Birmingham, Ala., which led to the arrest of 3,300 blacks. In the summer of 1963 he delivered his famous speech to the participants of the March on Washington. On 10 December 1964 he received the Nobel Peace Prize, and in early 1965 he led a voter-registration drive in Selma, Alabama, which occasioned the Selma-Montgomery March. In 1966, King went north to protest housing discrimination in Chicago, and during the last two years of his life he was a leader of the anti-Vietnam War Movement. In March 1968 he went to Memphis, Tennessee, to help the city's garbage men who were on strike. There he was assassinated on 4 April 1968.

Vocabulary

Intro/1 to stage (v.): to cause to happen, esp. for show or public effect - **Intro/2 civil rights** (n.): the non-political rights, such as freedom, equality, etc., which belong to persons because they are citizens and without regard to their race, religion, color, sex, etc. - **1 score** (n.): (often in combination) a group of 20 - **3 momentous** (adj.): of very great importance or seriousness - **3 decree** (n.): a judgment (of certain types) in a court of law - **4 beacon** (n.): s.o. or s.th. that provides guidance or sets a high standard to be followed - **5 to sear** (v.): /sɪə/ to burn with a sudden powerful heat; to dry up - **5 withering** (adj.): intended to make s.o. feel uncertain, ashamed, or completely without confidence - **10 manacle** (n.): /ˈmænəkəl/ (usually pl.) either of a pair of iron rings joined by a chain, used for fastening the hands or feet of a prisoner - **10 segregation** (n.): the separation of a social or esp. racial group from others, as by laws against using the same schools, hotels, buses, etc. - **14 prosperity** (n.): good fortune and success, esp. in money matters - **15 to languish** (v.): to be or become lacking in strength or will; to experience long suffering. The pres.part. would normally be used here. - **22 promissory** (adj.): /ˈprɒmɪsərɪ ‖ ˈprɑːmɪsɔːrɪ/ containing or conveying a promise - **25 unalienable** (adj.): also inalienable, that is, which cannot be taken away - **27 to default** (v.): to fail to fulfil a contract, agreement, or duty; esp. (+ on) to fail to pay a debt - **32 insufficient** (adj.): (esp. of power, money, or resources) not enough - **36 vaults** (n. pl.): /vɔːlts/ an underground room with thick walls and a heavy door to protect it against fire and thieves, in which money, etc., is kept (at a bank) - **41 to hallow** (v.): to make holy - **45 to tranquilize** (n.): to make calm or peaceful, usually by means of a drug - **45 gradualism** (n.): the policy of approaching a desired end step by step - **48 desolate** (adj.): (of a place) sad and without people in it - **50 quicksand** (n.): wet sand which pulls in any beings which try to cross it - **55 sweltering** (adj.): unpleasantly hot - **57 to invigorate** (v.): to give a feeling of freshness and healthy strength to - **60 rude** (adj.): sudden and unpleasant - **62 tranquility** (n.): the state of being pleasantly calm, quiet, or peaceful; the state of being free from anxiety, worry, etc. - **64 whirlwind** (n.): a tall pipe-shaped body of air moving forward while whirling at high speed - **66 to emerge** (v.): to come out or appear from inside or from being hidden - **68 threshold** (n.): the place or point of beginning - **78 to engulf** (v.): (of the earth, sea, etc.) to destroy by swallowing up - **82 to tie up with** (v.): to connect - **83 inextricable** (adj.): /ˌɪnɪkˈstrɪkəbəl/ which cannot be escaped from because it is so difficult; which cannot be untied or separated - **85 pledge** (n.): a solemn promise or agreement - **87 devotee** (n.): a person who admires s.o. or s.th.; a person who devotes him/herself to religion - **92 fatigue** (n.): great tiredness; exhaustion - **103 righteousness** (n.): (of people and behavior) the quality of (doing what is) lawful and morally good - **105 tribulation** (n.): (a cause of) trouble, grief, worry, suffering, etc. - **107 quest** (n.): a search, an attempt to find - **108 to batter** (v.): to damage, break, or cause to lose shape by continual hard use or beating; to beat hard and repeatedly - **108 persecution** (n.): the action of treating cruelly or causing to suffer, esp. for religious or political beliefs - **111 redemptive** (adj.): relating to or bringing about redemption - **116 to wallow** (v.): to move, roll, or lie about happily in deep mud, dirt, water, etc., as some animals do - **122 creed** (n.): a system of (e.g. religious) beliefs or principles - **137 vicious** (adj.): cruel, having or showing hate and the desire to hurt; dangerous, able or likely to cause severe hurt - **138 interposition** (n.): the act of interfering or intervention - **144 to exalt** (v.): to praise highly; to raise to a high rank - **146 crooked** (adj.): not straight, twisted, bent; dishonest - **151 to hew** (v.): /hjuː/ to cut s.th. with a cutting tool - **153 to jangle** (v.): to (cause to) make a sharp sound, like metal striking against metal; to excite unpleasantly, to upset - **160 thee** (pron.): (old use) you - **172 curvaceous** (adj.): /kɜː(r)ˈveɪʃəs/ having a well-proportioned figure marked by pronounced curves - **172 slope** (n.): a surface that slopes; a piece of ground going up or down - **177 molehill** (n.): a small heap of earth thrown up on the surface by a mole when it is digging underground - **180 hamlet** (n.): a small village - **183 Gentile** (n.): a person who is not Jewish

Explanations

3 Emancipation Proclamation: the proclamation issued by President Abraham Lincoln after the battle of Antietam in September 1862 to take effect on the following 1 January. The first draft declared all slaves in rebel territory to be free, while those in loyal or conquered states were to be freed by other legislation. As it was actually ineffective in the areas controlled by the Confederacy, the proclamation was largely an announcement of Lincoln's aims and policies. It was later reinforced by the 13th Amendment. - **138 nullification** (n.): The extremists of the state-rights theory argued that the Constitution reserved to the individual state all powers not specifically granted to the federal government. It was this belief that led John Cauldwell Calhoun to demand, in his "South Carolina Exposition" (1828), that the "United States is not a union of the people, but a league or compact between sovereign states, any of which has the right to judge when the compact is broken and to pronounce any law to be null and void which violates its conditions." It was this insistence on the individual state's right of 'nullification' that eventually led to secession. - **161 pilgrim** (n.): in November 1620, 102 'pilgrims,' who were Separatists opposing the episcopal jurisdiction, rites, and discipline of the Church of England, came to Massachusetts on the *Mayflower*. By extension not only these but all the early settlers of Plymouth Colony are called 'pilgrims.' - **168 Alleghenies** (n.): the central region of the Appalachian mountains in eastern North America - **170 Rockies** (n.): short for 'Rocky Mountains,' the major mountain system of West North America, extending more than 3,000 miles from central New Mexico to Northwest Alaska.

Background Reading

On 5 February 1964, Martin Luther King, Jr. gave a lecture on "The American Dream" at Drew University, Madison, New Jersey, in which he said:

> I would like to use as a subject from which to speak tonight, the American Dream. And I use this subject because America is essentially a dream, a dream yet unfulfilled. The substance of the dream is expressed in some very familiar words found in the Declaration of Independence. "We hold these truths to be self-evident: that all men are created equal; that they are endowed by their Creator with certain inalienable rights; that among these are life, liberty, and the pursuit of happiness." This is a dream. [...] But ever since the Founding Fathers of our nation dreamed this dream, America has been something of a schizophrenic personality, tragically divided against herself. On the one hand we have proudly professed the great principles of democracy. On the other hand we have sadly practiced the very antithesis of those principles. Indeed, slavery and racial segregation are strange paradoxes in the nation founded on the principle that all men are created equal. But now, more than ever before, our nation is challenged to realize this dream. For the shape of the world today does not afford us the luxury of an anemic democracy, and the price that America must pay for the continued oppression of the Negro and other minority groups is the price of its own destruction. The hour is late and the clock of destiny is ticking out, and we must act now before it is too late.

Thirty years after King's speech, *Time*, 30 October 1995, p. 40, could say this about African Americans:

> In the most heated political and policy debates of recent years, black men have seen themselves cast, sometimes openly, sometimes with a wink and a nod, as the welfare-freeloader, the affirmative-action hire, the inherently unintelligent, the repeat offender. Even worse than the stereotypes sometimes are the facts. For black men the average life expectancy is 65, eight years less than for white males. For young black men, the major cause of death is murder. Nearly 1 in every 3 black men between 20 and 29 years of age is behind bars, on probation or on parole.

Awareness

1 Collect what you know about the situation of African Americans in the U.S. of today.

Comprehension

2 What connection does King establish between "the Declaration of Independence" (l. 21), "a great American, in whose symbolic shadow we stand today" (ll. 1f.), and his own demands?
3 What is the relation between the promise of "five score years ago" (l. 1) and the reality of 1963?
4 To what extent can 1963 be "not an end but a beginning" (l. 58)?

Analysis

5 Define the particular meaning which the 'Dream' assumes in King's speech.

6 Identify and describe such strategies as parallelisms, repetitions, etc. which make King's speech such a moving example of powerful rhetoric.

7 Collect and analyze (a) the historical and (b) the Biblical allusions by means of which King relates his plea to the course of American history and the promises of Christian religion.

Opinion

8 Why do you think King's speech became so famous?

Projects

9 Study the short quotation from *Time*, October 1995, on p. 25 and assess the degree to which King's hopes as expressed in 1964 had become reality thirty years later. Try to find out about more recent developments. Some of the statistics in text 21 might help.

10 Analyze the complete text of King's speech on "The American Dream," which is available, with annotations, on the CD or in the internet under http://depts.drew.edu/lib/archives/online_exhibits/King/speech/TheAmericanDream.pdf), and relate it to "I Have a Dream."

11 Collect information about Malcolm X, listen to his famous "The Ballot or the Bullet" speech (available on the CD in the Resource Book to the Viewfinder Topic *New York: The Big Apple* as both an audio file and an annotated transcript), and contrast his position with King's course of non-violent action.

12 Compare King's speech with the speech given by Louis Farrakhan, the head of the Nation of Islam, in the same place on 16 October 1995 on the occasion of the Million Man March (http://www-cgi.cnn.com/US/9510/megamarch/10-16/transcript/).

Internet Project

13 Visit the website www.thekingcenter.com and gather further information about Martin Luther King, Jr. Prepare a Powerpoint presentation of the major events in which he played a leading role.

5

Langston Hughes

"Harlem"

Langston Hughes, an African American novelist, poet, and playwright, was born in Joplin, Missouri, attended Columbia University, and soon became a celebrated member of the Harlem Renaissance. His work includes several collections of short stories, five dramas, a novel, numerous volumes of poetry, and books, essays, and articles on social, historical, and musical subjects. – Langston Hughes, *Montage of a Dream Deferred* (New York: Henry Holt and Company, 1951), p. 71.

What happens to a dream deferred?

Does it dry up
like a raisin in the sun?
Or fester like a sore –
And then run?
Does it stink like rotten meat?
Or crust and sugar over –
like a syrupy sweet?

Maybe it just sags
like a heavy load.

Or does it explode?

Langston Hughes (1902-67) was born in Joplin, Missouri. In 1921 he entered Columbia University, but left to participate in the cultural activities in nearby Harlem, where he soon became a promising representative of the so-called Harlem Renaissance. His poems appeared in Alain Locke's seminal anthology *The New Negro;* in 1926 he published his first collection, *The Weary Blues*, and wrote an important critical essay on "The Negro Artist and the Racial Mountain;" and in 1930 his first novel, *Not Without Laughter*, won the Harmon Gold Award for Literature. During the 1930s, Hughes embraced radical politics and published a collection of satirical short stories, *The Ways of White Folks* (1934). Later he would again highlight the absurdities of racial prejudice in *Laughing to Keep from Crying* (1952) and *Something in Common* (1963). In 1935 his play *The Mulatto* was produced on Broadway, and he founded black theater groups in Harlem, Los Angeles, and Chicago. His dramatic work is collected in *Five Plays* (1963). Besides many other volumes of poetry, Hughes published two autobiographies, *The Big Sea* (1940) and *I Wonder as I Wander* (1956), and numerous books, essays, and articles on all kinds of subjects as well as collections of black folklore. In his later years he wrote the "Simple stories," which deal with a seemingly slow-witted black character who always outsmarts his antagonists and which are collected in four volumes from *Simple Speaks His Mind* (1950) to *Simple's Uncle Sam* (1965). Hughes' second novel, *Tambourines to Glory*, appeared in 1958.

Vocabulary

1 to defer (v.): to put off or hold back until a later date - **3 raisin** (n.): a sweet dried fruit (grape) used in cakes, bread, etc. - **4 to fester** (v.): (of a cut or wound) to become infected and diseased - **4 sore** (n.): a painful usually infected place on the body - **5 to run** (v.): of a (running) sore, to give out pus - **7 to crust over** (v.): to become covered with a hard usually brown outer surface - **8 syrupy** (adj.): of or like syrup, a sweet liquid, esp. sugar and water - **9 to sag** (v.): to sink, settle, or bend downward, esp. from the usual or correct position

Explanations

Intro/2 Harlem Renaissance (n.): The first major, self-conscious cultural movement of black American artists from the early 1920s through the early 1930s, which is also called the 'New Negro' or Black Renaissance. It found its center in Harlem and was infused by a new spirit of achievement and opportunity for collective creative expression by black writers, in contrast to the solitary efforts of earlier literary figures. The four major writers who established their reputation during this period were Claude McKay, Jean Toomer, Countee Cullen, and Langston Hughes.

Analysis

1 Define Hughes' criticism of the 'Dream' and contrast it with the hopes and beliefs of Martin Luther King, Jr.

2 Investigate in how far the structure and rhyme scheme of Hughes' poem support and enhance its message.

Opinion

3 Whose position, the hopeful one of King or the pessimistic one of Hughes, proves to be truer to the contemporary situation of African Americans? Give reasons for your answer.

Internet Project

4 Use http://www.prenhall.com/aahtour/harlem.html for a virtual tour of the Harlem Renaissance; http://www.nyc.gov/html/dcp/html/mxb/index.shtml for a virtual tour along Malcolm X Boulevard; or one of the many "tour of Harlem" videos provided on YouTube, and try to find out some basic facts about the complex history of Harlem.

Further Reading

5 Read and analyze Hughes' "Ballad of the Landlord" (available in P. Freese, ed., *New York Stories* [München: Langenscheidt, 1998 and ff., pp. 41ff.]).

6 Read Lorraine Hansberry's play *A Raisin in the Sun* (available in a school edition shortened and annotated by G. Hergt [Stuttgart: Klett, 1980 and ff.]), which takes its title from Hughes' poem.

6

Michael Drayton

"To the Virginian Voyage"

In December 1606, Christopher Newport sailed forth from England to bring 144 settlers to the British colony called Virginia in honor of Elizabeth I, the 'Virgin Queen.' The poet Michael Drayton celebrated this event in an ode which is a characteristic example of the European concept of America as an innocent and pastoral country that provides a stark contrast to a sinful and urbanized Europe. The settlers, however, who founded Jamestown on 13 May 1607 and who were threatened with extinction by disease, starvation, and hostile Indians during the winters of 1608 and 1609, would soon learn to reject this view as totally wrong. – *Poems of Michael Drayton*, ed. by John Buxton (London: Routledge and Kegan Paul, 1953), vol. I, pp. 123-125.

You brave heroique minds,
Worthy your countries name,
That honour still pursue,
Goe, and subdue,
Whilst loyt'ring hinds
Lurke here at home, with shame.

Britains, you stay too long,
Quickly aboord bestow you,
And with a merry gale
Swell your stretch'd sayle,
With vowes as strong,
As the winds that blow you.

[…]

And cheerefully at sea,
Successe you still intice,
To get the pearle and gold,
And ours to hold,
Virginia,
Earth's onely paradise.

Where nature hath in store,
Fowle, venison, and fish,
And the fruitfull'st soyle,
Without your toyle,
Three harvests more,
All greater than you wish.

And the ambitious vine
Crownes with his purple masse,
The Cedar reaching hie
To kisse the sky,
The Cypresse, pine
And use-full Sassafras.

To whose, the golden age
Still natures lawes doth give,
No other cares that tend,
But them to defend
From winters age,
That long there doth not live.

When as the lushious smell
Of that delicious land,
Above the seas that flowes,
The cleere wind throwes,
Your hearts to swell
Approaching the deare strand.

[…]

And in regions farre
Such heroes bring yee foorth,
As those from whom we came,
And plant our name,
Under that starre
Not knowne unto our north.

And as there plenty growes
Of lawrell every where,
Apollo's sacred tree,
You it may see,
A poets browes
To crowne, that may sing here.

Thy voyages attend,
Industrious Hackluit,
Whose reading shall inflame,
Men to seeke fame,
And much commend
To after-times thy wit.

Michael Drayton (1563-1631) was born at Hartshill, Warwickshire, in 1563 and spent his early years in the service of the Goodere family, to whom he owed his education. He produced a vast quantity of historical, topographical, and religious verse as well as odes, sonnets, and satires. His *Ideas Mirrour* (1594) is a series of sonnets, which includes the brilliant "Since there's no help, come let us kiss and part;" his most popular work in the seventeenth century, *England's Heroical Epistles* (1597), is a series of pairs of letters exchanged by famous lovers; his *Poemes Lyrick and Pastorall* (about 1605) contain the splendid "Ballad of Agincourt" ("Fair stood the wind for France") and the ode "To the Virginian Voyage;" and his *Polyolbion* (1622) is a great topographical poem on England. Drayton's best poetry is inspired by patriotism and by the enchantments found in English landscape and history.

Info

Ode

(Greek *aidein* "to sing," "to chant"). In modern usage the name for the most formal, ceremonious, and complexly organized form of lyric poetry, usually of considerable length. It is frequently the vehicle for public utterance on state occasions, as, for example, a ruler's birthday, accession, funeral, the unveiling or dedication of some imposing memorial or public work. The ode as it has evolved in contemporary literatures generally shows a dual inheritance from classic sources, combining the reflective or philosophic character of the Horatian ode with the occasional character of the Pindaric ode [...] The serious tone of the ode [...] calls for the use of a heightened diction and enrichment by poetic device [...] – *Princeton Encyclopedia of Poetry and Poetics.*

Vocabulary

Intro/4 pastoral (adj.): concerning simple and peaceful country life - **Intro/4 stark** (adj.): hard, bare, or severe in appearance; pure, complete - **Intro/4 to urbanize** (v.): to cause to take on urban characteristics - **1 heroique** (adj.): old form of 'heroic' - **3 to pursue** (v.): to continue (steadily) with, to be busy with - **4 Goe**: old form of the imperative 'go' - **4 to subdue** (v.): to conquer or control the actions of - **5 whilst** (conj.): old form of 'while' - **5 loyt'ring**: old pres. part. of 'to loiter,' to move on or about with frequent stops - **6 to lurke** (v.): old form of 'to lurk,' to wait in hiding. In modern English, the difficult phrase "Goe, and subdue, / Whilst loyt'ring hinds / Lurke here at home, with shame" might be rephrased as 'Go out and subdue (the world), while those who loiter behind wait around here at home and hide in shame (for not being courageous enough to join you)' - **8 aboord** (adv., prep.): old form of 'aboard' - **8 to bestow o.s.** (v.): archaic for to put up, to lodge, to quarter - **9 gale** (n.): a very strong wind - **10 sayle** (n.): old form of 'sail' - **11 vowe** (n.): old form of 'vow,' a solemn promise or declaration of intention - **14 cheereful** (adj.): old form of 'cheerful' - **15 successe** (n.): old form of 'success' - **15 to intice** (v.): old form of 'to entice,' to persuade s.o. to do s.th. - **16 pearle** (n.): old form of 'pearl' - **19 onely** (adj.): old form of 'only' - **21 fowle** (n.): old form of 'fowl,' a farmyard bird, esp. a hen; the meat of this, cooked as food - **21 venison** (n.): /'venɪzən/ the flesh of a deer as food - **22 soyle** (n.): old form of 'soil,' the top covering of the earth in which plants grow - **23 toyle** (n.): old form of 'toil,' hard or continuous work - **26 ambitious** (adj.): having a strong desire for success, power, wealth, etc.; showing or resulting from a desire to do s.th. difficult or s.th. that demands great effort or skill - **27 to crowne** (v.): old form of 'to crown' - **28 cedar** (n.): /'siːdə/ a tall evergreen tree with hard reddish sweet-smelling wood - **28 hie** (adj.): old form of 'high' - **29 to kisse** (v.): old form of 'to kiss' - **30 cypresse** (n.): old form of 'cypress,' a tree with dark green leaves and hard wood that does not lose its leaves in winter - **30 pine** (n.): any of several types of tall tree with sharp leaves that do not drop off in winter, found esp. in colder parts of the world - **31 use-full** (adj.): old form of 'useful' - **31 sassafras** (n.): (the dried outer covering of the root of) a small tree of Asia and North America, used for its taste to make a kind of tea - **32 to whose**: to them, that is, to the trees mentioned in the preceding stanza - **33 lawes** (n. pl.): old plural of 'law' - **34 to tend** (v.): (1) to have a tendency; be likely to (do or be s.th.); to do or be often or usually; (2) to take care of (a living thing); to look after - **38 lushious** (adj.): /'lʌʃəs/ old form of 'luscious,' having a very pleasant taste or smell; being sweet, ripe, or healthy - **41 cleere** (adj.): old form of

Philippe Galle, America *(1581)*

'clear' - **43 deare** (adj.): old form of 'dear' - **45 farre** (adv.): old form of 'far' - **46 yee** (pron.): old form of 'you,' used esp. when addressing more than one person, usually only as the subject of a sentence - **46 foorth** (adv.): old form of 'forth' (used esp. in the Bible or in literature after a verb) out, forward - **49 starre** (n.): old form of 'star' - **50 knowne** (adj.): old form of 'known' - **51 to growe** (v.): old form of 'to grow' - **52 lawrell** (n.): /'lɒrəl/ old form of 'laurel,' a small tree with smooth shiny dark green leaves that do not fall in winter; honor gained for s.th. done - **55 browes** (n.pl.): old form of '(eye)brows' - **56 to crowne** (v.): old form of 'to crown' - **59 to inflame** (v.): here to incite, to encourage - **60 to seeke** (v.): old form of 'to seek'

Explanations

Intro/2 Virginia: Named for Elizabeth I, the 'Virgin Queen,' 'Virginia' at first designated the whole vast area of North America not held by the Spanish or French. The first 'Lost Colony' on Roanoke Island organized by Sir Walter Raleigh in 1585 failed, with the fate of the settlers remaining a riddle to this day, but the English soon made a further attempt slightly farther north. In 1606, James I granted a charter to the London Company (later known as the Virginia Company), a group of merchants lured by the promise of easy profits in mining and the Indian trade. This company sent three ships and 144 men under Captains Christopher Newport, Bartholomew Gosnold, and John Ratcliffe to establish a base, and the tiny force entered Chesapeake Bay in April, 1607. On a peninsula in the James River they founded, on 13 May 1607, the first permanent English settlement in America, which they called Jamestown. Since the original plans soon turned out to be unrealistic, the settlers began their long struggle to live off the land, and by 1608, despite the firm and resourceful leadership of John Smith, hunger and disease had reduced their number to 38. - **32 golden age**: In classical mythology, the history of the world, as systematized by Hesiod and Ovid, was understood as a sequence of four ages. These were the Golden Age, the Silver Age, the Bronze Age, and the Iron Age, with the first, which was ruled by Cronus (Saturn), being a period of serenity, peace, and eternal spring. Hence the 'golden age' stands metaphorically for a period of time, either real or imaginary, when everyone was happy, the best work was done, etc. - **53 Apollo**: one of the most important Olympian gods in Greek mythology, who, as the patron of music and poetry, was often connected with the Muses - **58 Hackluit**: Richard Hakluyt (1522?-1616) dedicated most of his life to collecting and publishing the accounts of English explorations, and in his *Principall Navigations, Voiages, and Discoveries of the English Nation* (1589; much enlarged, in three volumes, 1598-1600), he collected accounts of almost all the important voyages, thus bringing to light the achievements of English navigators and greatly boosting discovery and colonization.

Awareness

1 In 1606, when Drayton wrote his ode, not much was known about the 'New World,' which was so huge and so wild that it defied the human imagination. Thus some dreamt of America as a new Garden of Eden, while others feared it as a dangerous and hellish place. Verbalize the message of the Flemish printmaker Philippe Galle's allegorical depiction of 'America' (p. 29) and comment on the hypothetical nature of the images of 'America' which people held in those days.

Comprehension

2 Transform stanzas four to seven of the poem as precisely as possible into a prose text in contemporary English.

3 List the characteristics which make Virginia "Earth's onely paradise" (l. 19).

Analysis

4 Investigate the way in which Drayton relates the concept of the 'golden age' to 'Virginia.'

5 Analyze Drayton's admonitions to his fellow "Britains" (l. 7) in the light of ll. 1-4, 8, 16-18, and 45-50. Relate the English 'empire building' mentality behind these calls to "plant our name" (l. 48) to the American position which Josiah Strong expounds in text 9.

Project

6 Use appropriate history books and encyclopaedias to collect information about the events in Jamestown during the first years of the colony and compare Drayton's wishful thinking to historical reality.

Internet Project

7 View the videos about the "Jamestown Settlement" (http://www1.teachertube.com/viewVideo.php?video_id=19705) and "The Jamestown Colony" (http://www.youtube.com/watch?v=ZINHFyVDp3s), and write a short essay on what you have learned about Jamestown.

7

George Berkeley

"On the Prospect of Planting Arts and Learning in America"

In 1726, the Irish philosopher George Berkeley wrote a poem about his plans to erect a college in the Bermuda Islands, which was to "convert the savage Americans to Christianity," and in 1729 he went to Rhode Island, where he tried in vain for almost three years to obtain money for his project. His plan never materialized, but when the College of California was moved from Oakland to Ocean View on the Eastern shore of San Francisco Bay, the trustees named both their institution and its new home town 'Berkeley' in honor of the man who had most clearly expressed the heliotropic idea of *translatio imperii, religionis et studii.* – *The Works of George Berkeley, Bishop of Cloyne,* ed. by A. A. Luce and T. E. Jessop (Nendeln: Kraus Reprint, 1979), vol. VII, p. 373.

The Muse, disgusted at an Age and Clime,
Barren of every glorious Theme,
In distant Lands now waits a better Time,
Producing Subjects worthy Fame:

In happy Climes, where from the genial Sun
And virgin Earth such Scenes ensue,
The Force of Art by Nature seems outdone,
And fancied Beauties by the true:

In happy Climes the Seat of Innocence,
Where Nature guides and Virtue rules,
Where Men shall not impose for Truth and Sense,
The Pedantry of Courts and Schools:

There shall be sung another golden Age,
The rise of Empire and of Arts,
The Good and Great inspiring epic Rage,
The wisest Heads and Noblest Hearts.

Not such as *Europe* breeds in her decay;
Such as she bred when fresh and young,
When heav'nly Flame did animate her Clay,
By future Poets shall be sung.

Westward the Course of Empire takes its Way;
The four first Acts already past,
A fifth shall close the Drama with the Day;
Time's noblest Offspring is the last.

Andrew Melrose, Westward the Star of Empire Takes Its Way – near Council Bluffs, Iowa, 1867

George Berkeley (1685-1753), was born at Dysert Castle, in Kilkenny County, and educated at Kilkenny and Trinity College, Dublin. In 1713 he came to England, where he became associated with Addison, Steele, Swift, and Pope. He was made dean of Derry in 1724, and bishop of Cloyne in 1734. In 1752 he retired to Oxford, where he died. Berkeley is best known as an idealistic philosopher criticizing John Locke's external, material reality. For him, only particular things exist, and since they are only a complex of sensations, nothing remains if we abstract from them that of which we have perception. The 'support' of ideas or sensations is the percipient mind, and therefore the *esse* of material things is *percipi*. Less known is Berkeley's abortive scheme of founding a college in Bermuda, for which he published "A Proposal for the better Supplying of Churches in our Foreign Plantations, and for Converting the Savage Americans, to Christianity, by a College to be erected in the *Summer Islands*, otherwise called *The Isles of Bermuda*" (1725), and also a poem (1726). This poem was not printed until 1752, but then it became immediately popular in America and was frequently quoted in newspapers and magazines.

George Caleb Bingham, Daniel Boone Escorting Settlers Through the Cumberland Gap (1851/52)

Vocabulary

Intro/8 heliotropic (adj.): characterized by or pertaining to heliotropism, that is, that property of an organism by virtue of which it tends, when not symmetrically illuminated on all sides, to move either toward or away from the source of light - **1 muse** (n.): an ancient Greek goddess, one of nine who each represented an art or science - **1 clime** (n.): poetic for 'climate' - **2 barren** (adj.): useless, empty, with no interest, which produces no result - **5 genial** (adj.): /'dʒiːnɪəl/ cheerful, friendly, and good-tempered - **6 to ensue** (v.): to happen afterwards (often as a result) - **11 to impose** (v.): to force the acceptance of (usually s.th. difficult or unwanted); to take unfair advantage, in a way that causes additional work and trouble - **12 pedantry** (n.): /'pedntrɪ/ the quality of being a pedant (a person who pays too much attention to small details and unimportant rules) - **15 epic** (adj.): (of stories, events, etc.) full of brave action and excitement - **19 to animate** (v.): to give life or excitement to; to enliven - **19 clay** (n.): heavy firm earth, soft when wet, becoming hard when baked at a high temperature - **24 offspring** (n.): a child or children

Explanations

Intro/8 ***translatio imperii***: see the extra information on page 33 - **13 golden Age**: see text 6, l. 32 - **22 the four first Acts**: If the history of the world is understood as a drama that unfolds in five Aristotelian acts, then - Berkeley argues - the first four have passed and the fifth is going to take place in the New World.

Info

Translatio imperii

This complex and highly influential concept has several roots. It is generally assumed that the idea of the westward movement of civilization came into being as an analogy to the course of the sun - *ex oriente lux* - as reinforced by the ancient metaphor of 'the light of reason.' Later, this widespread notion was combined with an influential Biblical tradition originating from chapters 2 and 7 of the Book of Daniel. Daniel's vision of the four beasts was interpreted by Christian historiographers such as Augustine and Orosius as a prophetic description of the divinely ordained course of history that was understood to unfold through a succession of the four great kingdoms of Babylonia, Media-Persia, Greece, and Rome and that was believed to find its predestined fulfilment in the crowning kingdom of God. Thereafter, this concept developed into competing national traditions, and in Germany, for example, the crowning of Charlemagne was thought to be proof of a fifth empire, namely, that of the Franks, and led to the notion of the *translatio imperii ad Teutonicos* as explained by Bishop Otto of Freising. This medieval notion resurfaced during the Reformation, when the German Protestants felt divinely ordained to replace the corrupt empire of Roman papacy. But other nations also appropriated the idea and combined it with notions of racial superiority, related the stages of world history to the five acts of a complete Aristotelian drama, and claimed central roles for themselves. Predictably, the concept of the westward progress of civilization acquired new momentum with the discovery of America, since now European Christians felt increasingly called upon to follow the light of the sun into hitherto unchartered regions, there to missionize the 'heathens' of an expanding world and thus to contribute to the power and glory of their own nation and to expedite not only the westward course of empire *(translatio imperii)*, but also of religion *(translatio religionis)* and of learning *(translatio studii)*.

Awareness

1 Berkeley was motivated by the well-meant attempt to bring Christianity and culture ("arts and learning") to the 'savages'. Describe the 'success' and/or 'failure' of such European missionizing and colonizing in the light of historical experience.

Comprehension

2 Contrast the characteristics which Berkeley ascribes to the promising new world and the worn-out old world respectively.

3 Sum up Berkeley's argument in your own words.

Analysis

4 Compare Berkeley's notion of "another golden Age" (l. 13) in America with Drayton's use of the same concept in l. 32 of text 6.

5 Investigate how Berkeley develops the contrast between Europe and America in terms of "art" versus "nature."

6 Re-read Berkeley's poem against the background of (a) the heliotropic notion of *translatio imperii* and (b) the Aristotelian notion of the unfolding of history in five acts.

7 Study Melrose's painting and describe the effects which the westward movement of the "star of empire" has on the 'natural' landscape of the New World.

Project

8 Collect and analyze, with the help of Information Sheet 6, other examples of the *translatio*-notion and trace its historical mutations.

9 Use the internet to collect information about Bingham's painting (http://www.tnhistoryforkids.org/students/4_history_3 offers interesting material for fourth-grade American students) and write a short essay about the meaning of the painting.

8 American Reactions to Berkeley's 'Prophecy'

On 3 September 1730, the *Boston Newsletter* printed an anonymous letter to the editor, which related the *translatio*-notion to the legend of the Pilgrim Fathers stepping ashore on Plymouth Rock and thus incorporated the European tradition into an American context.

Plimouth, Massachusetts

SIR,

As there hath been discovered in this our Town a very wonderful Phenomena, I have sent you an Account thereof for the Perusal of your curious Readers,

— Walking last Week with a Friend by a Place where they were about to dig a Cellar, we discovered a Stone, on which there seemed to be Engraven certain Letters, which when we had cleared from the Dirt, we read to our great Astonishment engraven very deep the ensuing Lines,

The Eastern World enslav'd, it's Glory ends;
and Empire rises where the Sun descends.

It seemeth to have been buried long in the Earth; but as I intend to bring it with me to Boston so soon as the Distemper is past, and shew it to the curious and learned Gentlemen in that Place, it seemeth unnecessary to give any further Description thereof at Present.

Your assured friend, &c.

Emanuel Leutze, Westward the Course of Empire Takes Its Way, *mural study, United States Capitol, 1861*

On 4 July 1771, Benjamin Franklin wrote a letter to Charles Wilson Peale, in which he used Berkeley's prophecy to confirm his belief in America's future. – *The Papers of Benjamin Franklin,* vol. XVIII, *January 1 through December 31, 1771*, ed. by William B. Willcox (New Haven and London: Yale University Press, 1974), p. 163.

The Arts have always travelled Westward, and there is no doubt of their flourishing hereafter on our side the Atlantic, as the number of wealthy Inhabitants shall increase, who may be able and willing suitably to reward them, since from several Instances it appears that our People are not deficient in Genius.

A nineteenth-century advertisement for McCormick Reapers

On 23 May 1807, the second president of the United States, John Adams, wrote a letter to Benjamin Rush about the *translatio*-notion and the tradition initiated by the anonymous letter to the *Boston Newsletter*. – *The Works of John Adams*, ed. by Charles Francis Adams (Boston: Little Brown, 1850-56), vol. IX, pp. 599f.

[...] now I have mentioned my brother Cranch, a gentleman of four-score, whose memory is better than mine, I will relate to you a conversation with him last evening. I asked him if he recollected the first line of a couplet whose second line was, "and empire rises where the sun descends." He paused a moment and said, –

The eastern nations sink, their glory ends,
and empire rises where the sun descends.

I asked him, if Dean Berkeley was the author of them. He answered no. The tradition was, as he had heard it for sixty years, that these lines were inscribed, or rather drilled, into a rock on the shore of Monument Bay in our old colony of Plymouth, and were supposed to have been written and engraved there by some of the first emigrants from Leyden, who landed at Plymouth. However this may be, I may add my testimony to Mr. Cranch's, that I have heard these verses for more than sixty years. I conjecture that Berkeley became connected with them, in my head, by some report that the bishop had copied them into some publication. There is nothing, in my little reading, more ancient in my memory than the observation that arts, sciences, and empire had travelled westward; and in conversation it was always added since I was a child, that their next leap would be over the Atlantic into America. [...]

Vocabulary

7 perusal (n.): (formal) the careful study of a text - **9 to engrave** (v.): to cut (words, pictures, etc.) on wood, stone, or metal - **10 ensuing** (adj.): following - **13 seemeth** (v.): old form of 'seems' - **14 distemper** (n.): archaic for disturbance or disorder - **14 to shew** (v.): old form of 'to show' - **36 deficient** (adj.): not containing or having enough of s.th. - **40 score** (n.): (often in combination) a group of 20 - **42 couplet** (n.): two lines of poetry, one following the other, that are of equal length and end in the same sound - **50 testimony** (n.): a formal statement that s.th. is true - **50 to conjecture** (v.): to form (an opinion) from incomplete or uncertain information - **54 leap** (n.): a big jump

Explanations

1 ***translatio imperii***: see p. 33 - **2 Pilgrim Fathers**: the group of English settlers who arrived on the *Mayflower* at Plymouth, Mass., in 1620 - **2 Plymouth Rock**: Upon their arrival at the coast of Massachusetts, the 'Pilgrim Fathers' did not, as legend has it, step ashore at the granite boulder of Plymouth Rock, which is now carefully protected from the tourists who in former days chipped away pieces of this rock as souvenirs. - **17 Benjamin Franklin**: see text 12 - **17 Charles Wilson Peale**: (1741-1827) a leading American portrait painter and the founder of the Pennsylvania Academy of Fine Arts - **37 John Adams**: (1735-1826) the second president of the U.S. (see text 8). Born in Braintree (now Quincy), Mass., he graduated from Harvard in 1755 and soon entered public life. He helped draft the *Declaration of Independence* and after serving as vice-president for two terms, he was elected to the presidency in 1796. - **37 Benjamin Rush**: (1745-1813): a Philadelphia physician, the surgeon-general of the Continental Army, and a member of the Continental Congress - **46 Dean Berkeley**: see text 7 - **50 Monument Bay** (n.): that part of the Massachusetts coast where Plymouth Rock can be found - **49 Leyden**: the city in the Netherlands to which a small group of English separatists had fled in 1608. When the *Mayflower* set out for America, 35 of its 102 passengers were 'Saints' from Leyden, and they prevailed over the others, called the 'Strangers,' and remained the moving force behind the emigration.

Background Reading

In 1725, the tavern keeper, physician, and astronomer **Nathaniel Ames** (1708-64) from Dedham, Mass., began to publish **An Astronomical Diary**, which soon became the most popular almanac in colonial New England. In the 1758 volume, Ames commented on the progress of civilization in the New World and also employed the notion of *translatio imperii* to prophesy great things for "the Future State of North America." - *The Essays, Humor, and Poems of Nathaniel Ames*, ed. by Samuel Briggs (Cleveland: Short & Forman, 1891), pp. 285f.

Here we find a vast Stock of proper Materials for the Art and Ingenuity of Man to work upon: -Treasures of immense Worth; conceal'd from the poor ignorant aboriginal Natives! The Curious have observ'd that the Progress of Humane Literature (like the Sun) is from the East to the West; thus has it travelled thro' Asia and Europe, and now is arrived at the Eastern Shore of America. As the Coelestial Light of the Gospel was directed here by the Finger of GOD, it will doubtless, finally drive the long! long! Night of Heathenish Darkness from America: - So Arts and Sciences will change the Face of Nature in their Tour from Hence over the Appalachian Mountains to the Western Ocean; and as they march thro' the vast Desert, the Residence of Wild Beasts will be broken up, and their obscene Howl cease for ever; - Instead of which the Stones and Trees will dance together at the Music of Orpheus, - the Rocks will disclose their hidden Gems, - and the inestimable Treasures of Gold & Silver be broken up. Huge Mountains of Iron Ore are already discovered; and vast Stores are reserved for future Generations: This Metal more useful than Gold and Silver, will imploy Millions of Hands, not only to form the martial Sword, and peaceful Share, alternately; but an Infinity of Utensils improved in the Exercise of Art, and Handicraft amongst Men. Nature thro' all her Works has stamp'd Authority on this Law, namely, "That all fit Matter shall be improved to its best Purposes." - [...] O! Ye unborn Inhabitants of America! Should this Page escape its destin'd Conflagration at the Year's End, and these Alphabetical Letters remain legible, - when your Eyes behold the Sun after he has rolled the Seasons round for two or three Centuries more, you will know that in Anno Domini 1758, we dream'd of your Times.

Analysis

1. Investigate for each of the three texts on pp. 34f. (a) how it popularizes the notion of *translatio imperii*, (b) whether, and if so how, it refers to Berkeley's poem (text 7), and (c) how it modifies the original concept to fit American interests.
2. Analyze the additional text by Ames above in the light of the *translatio*-tradition.
3. Translate the message of Leutze's painting into a verbal description which pays attention to all the details.
4. Analyze the strategies which Leutze employs in his attempt at expressing the westward course of empire by means of a composite pictorial representation.
5. Compare Leutze's painting with the advertisement for McCormick Reapers and investigate what happens when a shared cultural concept is commercialized.

9

Josiah Strong

Our Country

In 1885, Josiah Strong, a Congregational minister and a fervent believer in Anglo-Saxon superiority, became a national figure when he wrote a bestseller for the American Home Missionary Society. In his book, he, too, took recourse to the tradition of *translatio imperii* and argued that America's destiny would be fulfilled by the Anglo-Saxon master race in the endless expanse of the American West. – Josiah Strong, *Our Country: Its Possible Future and Its Present Crisis*, ed. by Jurgen Herbst (Cambridge, Mass.: The Belknap Press of Harvard University Press, 1963), pp. 39f. and 200ff.

F.F. Palmer, Across the Continent: Westward the Course of Empire Takes Its Way *(1869)*

Since prehistoric times, populations have moved steadily westward, as De Tocqueville said, "as if driven by the mighty hand of God." And following their migrations, the course of empire, which Bishop Berkeley sang, has westward taken its way. The world's scepter passed from Persia to Greece, from Greece to Italy, from Italy to Great Britain, and from Great Britain the scepter is to-day departing. It is passing on to "Greater Britain," to our Mighty West, there to remain, for there is no further West; beyond is the Orient. Like the star in the East which guided the three kings with their treasures westward until at length it stood still over the cradle of the young Christ, so the star of empire, rising in the East, has ever beckoned the wealth and power of the nations westward, until today it stands still over the cradle of the young empire of the West, to which the nations are bringing their offerings. The West is today an infant, but shall one day be a giant, in each of whose limbs shall unite the strength of many nations.

[...]

The Anglo-Saxon is the representative of two great ideas, which are closely related. One of them is that of civil liberty. [...] The other [...] is that of a pure *spiritual* Christianity. [...] these are the forces which, in the past, have contributed most to the elevation of the human race, and they must continue to be, in the future, the most efficient ministers to its progress. It follows, then, that the Anglo-Saxon, as the great representative of these two ideas, [...], sustains peculiar relations to the world's future, is divinely commissioned to be, in a peculiar sense, his brother's keeper. [...] it is possible that, by the close of the next century, the Anglo-Saxons will out-number all the other civilized races of the world. Does it not look as if God were not only preparing in our Anglo-Saxon civilization the die with which to stamp the peoples of the earth, but as if he were also massing behind that die the mighty power with which to press it? My confidence that this race is eventually to give its civilization to mankind is not based on mere numbers – China forbid! I look forward to what the world has never yet seen united in the same race; viz., the greatest number, *and* the highest civilization.

There can be no reasonable doubt that North America is to be the great home of the Anglo-Saxon, the principal seat of his power, [...] America is to have the great preponderance of numbers and of wealth, and by the logic of events will follow the scepter of controlling influence. [...] It seems to me that God, with infinite wisdom and skill, is training the Anglo-Saxon race for an hour sure to come in the world's future. Heretofore there has always been in the history of the world a comparatively unoccupied land westward, into which the crowded countries of the East have poured their surplus populations. But [...] there are no more new worlds. The unoccupied arable lands of the earth are limited, and will soon be taken. The time is coming when the pressure of population on the means of subsistence will be felt here as it is now felt in Europe and Asia. Then will the world enter upon a new stage of its history – *the final competition of races, for which the Anglo-Saxon is being schooled.* [...] Whether the extinction of inferior races before the advancing Anglo-Saxon seems to the reader sad or otherwise, it certainly appears probable.

Josiah Strong (1847-1916) was born in Napierville, Illinois, graduated from Western Reserve College of Hudson, Ohio, and then went to Lane Theological Seminary in Cincinnati, where he became acquainted with the evangelical enthusiasm of Lyman Beecher. It was as Secretary for the Congregational Home Missionary Society in Ohio that Strong wrote *Our Country: Its Possible Future and Its Present Crisis.* The book was published in 1885 and brought its author national success.
As a crucial historical document, *Our Country* mirrors the beliefs of a dominant segment of American society at the end of the nineteenth century. It assumes that Protestant America is predestined to become God's special instrument in the regeneration of the world and argues that, in order to play this role, it must solve formidable problems in the growing cities of the East as well as in the newly settled West. Among the major tasks are the conquering of "heathen" Indians, the rejection or conversion of "infidel Papists," the defeating of the Mormons, and the missionizing of agnostic rationalists. Strong is not only an apostle of the social gospel movement, but also a fervent believer in the superiority of the Anglo-Saxon race, a belief he sees confirmed by the Social Darwinist tenet of the 'survival of the fittest.' Consequently, in *Our Country* he combines his plea for home missionizing in the West with a vision of a Protestant American republic as the embodiment of Christian Anglo-Saxon civilization and as a model for the world, carrying the concept of 'Manifest Destiny' to such an extreme that he not even shrinks back from calling for the dispossession of so-called 'weaker races.'

Vocabulary

Intro/1 fervent (adj:): feeling or showing strong and warm feelings - **Intro/3 to take recourse to** (v.): to turn to when in need of help - **6 scepter** (n.): a short rod carried by a ruler on ceremonial occasions as a sign of power - **14 to beckon** (v.): to make a silent sign, as with the finger, to call (s.o.) - **19 limb** (n.): a leg, arm, or wing of an animal - **25 elevation** (n.): the act of elevating, that is, of making finer, higher, or more educated - **30 to sustain** (v.): to keep in existence over a long period; to maintain - **32 to commission** (v.): to place a special order for, or to appoint s.o. to do s.th. - **40 die** (n.): a metal block used for shaping metal, plastic, etc. - **41 to stamp** (v.): to mark (a pattern, sign, etc.) on (an object or surface) by pressing - **42 to mass** (v.): to gather together in large numbers - **48 viz.** (adv.): (short for *videlicet*) that is to say - **53 preponderance** (n.): the state of being greater in amount, number, etc. - **57 heretofore** (adv.): until now; before this time - **61 surplus** (adj.): /'sɜː(r)pləs/ (an amount) additional to what is needed or used - **62 arable** (adj.): /'ærəbəl/ (of land) suitable or used for growing crops - **65 subsistence** (n.): the ability to live, esp. with little money or food; living with the smallest amount (of food or money) necessary - **69 extinction** (n.): the state of being or becoming extinct, that is, no longer existing

Explanations

Intro/1 Congregationalism: a form of church government in which each congregation or local church has free control of its own affairs, and bishops and presbyteries are eliminated. Many Congregational churches were established in the newly opened frontier regions and in 1826 the American Home Missionary Society was formed, for which Strong wrote his book. - **2 Alexis de Tocqueville**: (1805-59) a French politician and writer, whose observations made during a government mission to the U.S. resulted in *De la démocratie en Amérique* (2 vols., 1835; translated as *Democracy in America*, 4 vols., 1835-40), one of the classics of political literature. Tocqueville was a liberal deeply committed to human freedom, and he believed that political democracy and social equality would inevitably replace the aristocratic institutions of Europe. Consequently, he analyzed the American attempt to have both liberty and equality with regard to what Europe might learn from it. - **4 Bishop Berkeley**: see text 7 - **11 the three kings** (n.): According to Matthew 2, magi or wise men of the east, guided by the star of Bethlehem, came to adore the newborn Jesus. Christian tradition has set their number at three, called them kings, and given them the names of Caspar, Melchior, and Balthazar.

Background Reading

[...] if this nation is, in the providence of God, destined to lead the way in the moral and political emancipation of the world, it is time she understood her high calling, and were harnessed to the work. [...] It's equally plain that the religious and political destiny of our nation is to be decided in the West. There is the territory, and there soon will be the population, the wealth, and the political power. [...] the West is destined to be the great central power of the nation, and under heaven, must affect powerfully the cause of free institutions and the liberty of the world. The West is a young empire of mind, and power, and wealth, and free institutions, rushing up to a giant manhood, with a rapidity and a power never before witnessed below the sun. And if she carries with her the elements of her preservation, the experiment will be glorious - the joy of the nation - the joy of the whole earth, as she rises in the majesty of her intelligence and benevolence, and enterprise, for the emancipation of the world.

Lyman Beecher, "A Plea for the West" (1832)

If any young man is about to commence the world, with little in his circumstances to prepossess him in favor of one section more than another, we say to him, publicly and privately, Go to the West; there your capacities are sure to be appreciated, and your industry and energy rewarded.

Horace Greeley in the *New Yorker*, 25 August 1838

Why, were other reasons wanting, in favor of now elevating this question of the reception ofTexas into the Union, out of the lower region of our past party dissensions, up to its proper level of a high and broad nationality, it surely is to be found, found abundantly, in the manner in which other nations have undertaken to intrude themselves into it, between us and the proper parties to the case, in a spirit of hostile interference against us, for the avowed object of thwarting our policy and hampering our power, limiting our greatness and checking the fulfilment of our manifest destiny to overspread the continent allotted by Providence for the free development of our yearly multiplying millions.

John L. O'Sullivan, "Annexation," *United States Magazine and Democratic Review 17* (1845)

American development has exhibited not merely advance along a single line, but a return to primitive conditions on a continually advancing frontier line, and a new development for that area. American social development has been continually beginning over again on the frontier. This perennial rebirth, this fluidity of American life, this expansion westward with its new opportunities, its continuous touch with the simplicity of primitive society, furnish the forces dominating American character. The true point of view in the history of this nation is not the Atlantic coast, it is the Great West. Even the slavery struggle [...] occupies its important place in American history because of its relation to westward expansion.

In this advance, the frontier is the outer edge of the wave – the meeting point between savagery and civilization. [...] The frontier is the line of most rapid and effective Americanization. The wilderness masters the colonist. It finds him a European in dress, industries, tools, modes of travel, and thought. It takes him from the railroad car and puts him in the birch canoe. It strips off the garments of civilization and arrays him in the hunting shirt and the moccasin. It puts him in the log cabin of the Cherokee and Iroquois and runs an Indian palisade around him [...] Thus the advance of the frontier has meant a study movement away from the influence of Europe, a growth of independence on American lines. But the most important effect of the frontier has been in the promotion of democracy here and in Europe.

Frederick Jackson Turner, "The Significance of the Frontier in American History" (1893).

Awareness

1 Both Horace Greeley's injunction "Go West, young man" and Josiah Strong's praise of "our Mighty West" (l. 9) imply that in their days the West offered advantages. What were these advantages?

Comprehension

2 What is the difference between a European /'frʌntɪə/ and the American /frʌn'tɪr/?
3 Find a headline for each of the three paragraphs of Strong's text.
4 What connection does Strong establish between the star of Bethlehem and "the star of empire" (l. 13)?
5 What are the "two great ideas" (ll. 21f.) represented by the Anglo-Saxons?
6 Why can Lyman Beecher argue that "the religious and political destiny of our nation is to be decided in the West" (l. 3)?
7 What does Strong predict with regard to "the final competition of races" (l. 67)?

Analysis

8 What, with Turner, is the connection between frontier life and "the promotion of democracy" (l. 38)?
9 Why does Turner see the American frontier as "the line of most rapid and effective Americanization" (l. 32).
10 Define Strong's notion of the Anglo-Saxon race and its God-given tasks.
11 Relate Strong's text to the notions of the "frontier" (Turner) and "manifest destiny" (O'Sullivan).

Opinion

12 Explain why you agree or disagree with Turner's contention that "the true point of view" (l. 28) in American history "is not the Atlantic coast" but "the Great West" (ll. 28f.).
13 Write a short text in which you state your reasons for accepting or rejecting Strong's position.

Projects

14 Point out frontier elements that have survived till today.
15 Compare Strong's text with the Currier & Ives chromolithograph on p. 37 and with John Gast's painting *American Progress* on p. 42.
16 Relate Strong's brand of nationalism to the Anglo-Saxon racialism of Madison Grant (see text 7 in the Viewfinder Topic *From Melting Pot to Multiculturalism*).

10 Senator Albert J. Beveridge

"The Star of Empire"*

What happened to Berkeley's notion of the westward movement of empire when it became a catchphrase for imperialistic policy, is most evident in the speeches which Senator Albert J. Beveridge from Indiana made around the turn of the century about what America should do with regard to the Philippines. – Albert J. Beveridge, *The Meaning of the Times and Other Speeches* (Indianapolis: Bobbs-Merrill, 1908), pp. 118f.; 84f.

In his Republican Campaign Speech on "The Star of Empire" on 25 September 1900 in Chicago

"Westward the Star of Empire takes its Way." Not the star of kingly power, for kingdoms are everywhere dissolving in the increasing rights of men; not the star of autocratic oppression, for civilization is brightening and the liberties of people are broadening under every flag. But the star of empire, as Washington used the word, when he called this Republic an "empire"; as Jefferson understood it, when he declared our form of government ideal for extending "our empire" [...] This is the "empire" of which the prophetic voice declared "Westward the Star of Empire takes its Way" – the star of the empire of liberty and law, of commerce and communication, of social order and the Gospel of our Lord – the star of the empire of the civilization of the world. Westward *that* star of empire takes its course. And to-day it illumines our path of duty across the Pacific into the islands and lands where Providence has called us. [...] It is not true, as the Opposition asserts, that every race without instruction and guidance is naturally self-governing. If so, the Indians were capable of self-government. America belonged to them whether they were or were not capable of self-government. If they were capable of self-government it was not only wrong, but it was a crime to set up our independent government on their land without their consent. If this is true, the Puritans, instead of being noble, are despicable characters; and the patriots of 1776, to whom the Opposition compares the Filipinos, were only a swarm of land pirates. If the Opposition is right, the Zulus who owned the Transvaal were capable of self-government; and the Boers who expelled them, according to the opposition, deserve the abhorrence of righteous men.

In his speech on "Our Philippine Policy" on 9 January 1900 in the U.S. Senate

Mr. President, this question [of the Philippines] is deeper than any question of party politics; deeper than any question of the isolated policy of our country; deeper than any question of constitutional power. It is elemental. It is racial. God has not been preparing the English-speaking and Teutonic peoples for a thousand years for nothing but vain and idle self-contemplation and self-admiration. No! He has made us the master organizers of the world to establish system where chaos reigns. He has given us the spirit of progress to overwhelm the forces of reaction throughout the earth. He has made us adepts in government that we may administer government among savage and senile peoples.

Were it not for such a force as this the world would relapse into barbarism and night. And of all our race He has marked the American people as His chosen Nation finally to lead in the regeneration of the world. This is the divine mission of America, and it holds for us all profit, glory, happiness possible to man. We are trustees of the world's progress, guardians of its righteous peace. The judgment of the Master is upon us: "Ye have been faithful over a few things; I will make you ruler over many things."

What shall history say of us? Shall it say that we renounced that holy trust, left the savage to his base condition, the wilderness to the reign of waste, deserted duty, abandoned glory, forgot our sordid profit even, because we feared our strength and read the charter of our powers with the doubter's eye and the quibbler's mind? Shall it say that, called by events to captain and command the ablest, noblest race of history in one of history's largest works, we declined that great commission? Our fathers would not have had it so. No! They founded no paralytic government, incapable of the simplest act of administration. They planted no sluggard people, passive while the world's work calls. They established no reactionary Nation. They unfurled no retreating flag.

Senator Beveridge (1862-1927)

In his introduction to the 1908 edition of Senator Beveridge's speeches, **Albert Shaw** had this to say:

"Mr. Beveridge was elected to the United States Senate from the State of Indiana in January, 1899. He was thirty-six years old, had practiced law for about twelve years, and had held no public offices. [...] We had only then concluded our treaty of peace with Spain and acquired the Philippines. Our problems of colonial administration were bound to give us much concern, and to occupy a leading place in the discussions of Congress, as well as in the Presidential campaign of the following year. It was characteristic of Mr. Beveridge that he should have determined not to take his seat in the Senate until he was as well qualified to speak on those questions as any other man in the body. Not only did he prepare himself by a study of the legal and constitutional questions involved [...], but he resolved to go to the far East, see what we had taken upon ourselves in the Philippine archipelago, and also acquaint himself with the politics and conditions of Japan and China, and of the Russians in the far East. [...]Those who read these addresses will feel that they have before them the utterances of a man entitled to be placed in the statesman's class."

Vocabulary

Intro/2 catchphrase (n.): a phrase, often with little meaning, which becomes popular for a time so that everyone uses it - **17 to illumine** (v.): poetic for 'to illuminate' - **19 providence** (n.): (an act or event showing) God's care or the kindness of fate - **27 despicable** (adj.): /dɪ'spɪkəbəl/ deserving to be despised; contemptible - **33 abhorrence** (n.): the feeling or state of abhorring, that is, of hating very much, of detesting - **45 to overwhelm** (v.): to defeat or make powerless (usually a group of people) by much greater force of numbers - **47 adept** (n.): /'ædept/ a person who is adept, that is, highly skilled, at s.th. - **50 to relapse** (v.): (+ into) to fall back into a bad state of health or way of life; to return - **54 trustee** (n.): a person or firm that holds and controls property or money for the advantage of s.o. else; a member of a group appointed to control the affairs of a company, college, or other organization - **60 to renounce** (v.): to say formally that one has no more connection with - **60 trust** (n.): care; responsibility - **61 base** (adj.): esp. literary (of people, actions, etc.) showing a complete lack of moral principles; dishonorable - **62 sordid** (adj.): wicked and dishonorable; not noble - **64 quibbler** (n.): s.o. who quibbles, that is, argues about small unimportant points or details - **67 to decline** (v.): to refuse (a request or offer); to express unwillingness - **68 commission** (n.): a special job, duty, or power, given to a person or group of people - **69 paralytic** (adj.): suffering from paralysis, that is, from a loss or lack of ability to move, operate, think, etc. - **70 sluggard** (adj.): literary for habitually lazy - **72 to unfurl** (v.): to unroll and open (a flag, sail, etc.)

Explanations

8 George Washington: (1732-99) The first president of the U.S. came from a Virginia family, received only an elementary education, and embarked early upon a military career. In 1759 he married and settled down on his inherited Mount Vernon estate, leading the life of a country gentleman and serving in the Virginia House of Burgesses. But the conflict with Great Britain drew him into larger colonial politics, and he was a member of both Continental Congresses. Upon the outbreak of the Revolutionary War he was appointed commander-in-chief of the Continental Army, but after the final victory over the British troops at Yorktown, he retired to Mount Vernon. Soon, however, he returned to public affairs, served as president of the Federal Constitutional Convention, and was then elected president of the U.S. for two terms from 1789 to 1797. - **9 Thomas Jefferson**: see text 2, l. 119 - **11 the prophetic voice**: a reference to Bishop Berkeley (see text 7), whose poem is retrospectively read as an early prophecy of expansionist policy - **30 Zulus**: Zululand, the historic home of the Nguni-speaking Zulus, is now in the northeast of Natal, a province of the Republic of South Africa. When the Boers moved into Natal on their Great Trek, the Zulu chief Dingaan ambushed and slaughtered 500 of them in 1838, and in revenge about 3,000 Zulus were killed by Andries Pretorius and his forces in the Battle of Blood River. In 1843, the British succeeded the Boers and fought for a long time with the rebellious Zulus, conquering them in 1879. In 1887 they annexed Zululand and in 1897 made it part of Natal. In accordance with the Bantu Self-Government Act of 1959, the Union of South Africa designated a Zulu homeland called Kwazulu, which is made up of isolated tracts of land, only a few of which were part of historic Zululand. - **31 Transvaal**: The Transvaal (the land beyond the Vaal River) was inhabited by Bantu-speaking Africans, when the Boers arrived on their Great Trek (1835/36), forced out most of the Africans, and scattered over the huge territory, which later became a province of the Union of South Africa, with Pretoria as capital and Johannesburg as the largest city. - **32 Boers**: /bɔːz ‖ 'bəʊəz/ (Dutch: farmers) the inhabitants of South Africa of Dutch or French Huguenot descent, also known as Afrikaners. They first settled in what is today Cape Province, but when this territory was annexed by Britain in 1806, many of the Boers set out on the Great Trek (1835/36) and created new republics in Natal, the Transvaal, and the Orange Free State. After the South African War between the Boers and the British (1899-1902), the Boer territories were annexed and later became provinces of the Union of South Africa. - **56 "Ye have been ..."**: A quotation from the Biblical parable about the master who gives his servants some money according to their respective merits before he leaves for a journey and who, upon returning home, judges them according to what they have done with it. To the two who have doubled it, he says: "Well done, thou good and faithful servant; thou hast been faithful over a few things, I will make thee ruler over many things: enter thou into the joy of thy lord." (Matthew 25:21 and 23)

Comprehension

1 How does Beveridge justify the colonization of the territories inhabited by Native Americans, Filipinos, and Zulus?
2 What is, according to Beveridge, "the divine mission of America" (l. 53)?

Analysis

3 Investigate and define the change of meaning which the concept of 'the westward course of empire' has undergone from Berkeley to Beveridge.

Opinion

4 If you feel that Beveridge's claims to Anglo-Saxon racial superiority, divine election, and 'exceptionalism' are wrong, collect arguments with which to refute such claims.
5 Comment on whether the idea developed through texts 6 to 10 provide a (partial) explanation of American interventionism in Korea, Vietnam, Grenada, Panama, Iraq, Afghanistan, etc.

Projects

6 Use Walt Whitman's poem "Looking West from California's Shore" (available in most anthologies) as the starting point for an investigation of the political context within which the notion of 'manifest destiny' was extended beyond the boundaries of the American continent.
7 Write a paper in which you review the successive meanings of the *translatio imperii* concept from Berkeley through the Plymouth Rock couplet, Franklin's and Adams' letters and Ames' almanac to Strong and Beveridge.

11

John Gast

American Progress

In 1872, John Gast completed his famous painting *American Progress* to the specifications of the New York firm of George A. Crofutt. Crofutt, who would later use Gast's painting as a frontispiece for his travel guidebooks, had the painting reproduced as a 12 x 16 chromolithograph, which sold for $10 and bore a detailed explanation of the painting's symbolism on the reverse side.

American Progress! Subject, The United States of America

This rich and wonderful country - the progress of which at the present time, is the wonder of the old world - was, until recently, inhabited exclusively by the lurking savage and wild beasts of prey. If the rabid progress of the "Great West" has surprised our people, what will those of other countries think of the "Far West," which is destined, at an early day, to be the vast granary, as it is now the great treasure chamber of our country? How this change has been wrought, and by whom is illustrated by our Chromo, "American Progress."

Purely National in design, this beautiful painting represents the United States' portion of the American continent in its beauty and variety, from the Atlantic to the Pacific Ocean, illustrating at a glance the grand drama of Progress in the civilization, settlement and history of our own happy land.

In the foreground the central and principal figure, a beautiful and charming Female, is floating Westward through the air bearing on her forehead the "Star of Empire." She has left the cities of the East far behind, crossed the Alleghanies and the "Father of Waters," and still her march is Westward. In her right hand she carries a book - Common schools - the emblem of Education and the testimonial of our National enlightenment, while with the left hand she unfolds and stretches the slender wires of the Telegraph, that are to flash intelligence throughout the land. On the right of the picture is a city, steamships, manufactories, schools and churches, over which beams of light are streaming and filling the air - indicative of civilization. The general tone of the picture on the left declares darkness, waste and confusion. From the city proceed the three great continental lines of railway, passing the frontier settler's rude cabin, and extending toward the Western Ocean. Next to these are the transportation wagons, overland stage, hunters, gold seekers, pony express, the pioneer emigrant and the war dance of the "noble red man." Fleeing from "Progress," and towards the blue waters of the Pacific, which shows itself on the left of the picture beyond the snow-capped summits of the Sierra Nevadas, are the Indians, buffaloes, wild horses, bears and other game, moving Westward, ever Westward the Indians with their squaws, papooses, and "pony lodges," turn their despairing faces towards, as they flee from the presence of, the wonderous vision. The "Star" is too much for them.

What American man, woman or child does not feel a heartthrob of exultation as they think of the glorious achievements of Progress since the landing of the Pilgrim Fathers, on staunch old Plymouth Rock! What home, from the miner's humble cabin to the stately marble mansion of the capitalist, should be without this Great National Picture, which illustrates in the most artistic manner all the gigantic results of American Brains and Hands! Who would not have such a beautiful token to remind them of our country's grandeur and enterprise which have caused the mighty wilderness to blossom like the rose!!! One of the best art critics has pronounced this picture "one of the grandest conceptions of the age."

Vocabulary

3 to lurk (v.): to wait somewhere quietly and secretly, usu. because you are going to do s.th. wrong - **3 beast of prey** (n.): a bird or animal which lives by killing and eating other animals - **3 rabid** (adj.): here violent, furious - **5 granary** (n.): a place where grain, esp. wheat, is stored - **13 testimonial** (n.): s.th. that is given or done to s.o. to thank or praise them, or show admiration for them - **14 slender** (adj.): thin in an attractive or graceful way - **16 indicative** (adj.): to be a clear sign that a particular situation exists or that s.th. is likely to be true - **22 game** (n.): wild animals, birds, and fish that are hunted for food, esp. as a sport - **23 papoose** (n.) a young child of Native American parents; a sort of bag fixed to a frame, used for carrying a baby on a person's back - **25 heartthrob** (n.) a specific type of heartbeat that occurs when feeling strong emotions - **29 token** (n.): s.th. that represents a feeling, fact, event, etc.

Explanations

6 Chromo: short for chromolithograph, an image printed in colors by lithography and produced by hand separation of the colors - **12 Alleghanies**: a range of mountains which go from Virginia to Pennsylvania in the eastern U.S., and are part of the Appalachians - **12 Father of Waters**: a poetic term for the Mississippi River - **13 Common schools**: The Common School movement, ensuring that every child could receive a basic education funded by local taxes, was spearheaded by Horace Mann (1796-1859), the 'Father of the Common School', who, as the Secretary of the newly created Massachusetts Board of Education, worked for his belief that political stability and social harmony depended on education. - **21 Sierra Nevada**: a mountain range in California - **23 pony lodge**: a small hut in which horses are kept

12 Benjamin Franklin

"Advice to a Young Tradesman, Written by an Old One. To My Friend A.B."

In 1748, Benjamin Franklin published an American edition of an English manual for young tradesmen, entitled *The Instructor, or Young Man's Best Companion*. In order to adapt this manual to the American situation, he omitted several items and added others, including a short essay, which has become one of the classic texts of American success literature. Franklin's belief that "time is money" also finds strong expression in his autobiography, in which he presents his famous daily time table. – *The Papers of Benjamin Franklin*, ed. by Leonard W. Labaree et al. (New Haven: Yale University Press, 1961), vol. III, pp. 306-308; and *The Autobiography of Benjamin Franklin*, ed. by Leonard W. Labaree et al. (New Haven: Yale University Press, 1964), p. 154.

Currier & Ives, The Ladder of Success

The Precept of Order requiring that *every Part of my Business should have its allotted Time*, one Page in my little Book contain'd the following Scheme of Employment for the Twenty-four Hours of a natural Day.

The morning question, What good shall I do this day?	5, 6, 7	Rise, wash, and address *Powerful Goodness*; contrive day's business and take the resolution of the day; prosecute the present study; and breakfast.
	8, 9, 10, 11	Work
	12, 1	Read or overlook my accounts, and dine.
	2, 3, 4, 5	Work
Evening question, What good have I done today?	6, 7, 8, 9	Put things in their places, supper, music, or diversion, or conversation; examination of the day.
	10, 11, 12, 1, 2, 3, 4	Sleep

Advice to a Young Tradesman

As you have desired it of me, I write the following Hints, which have been of Service to me, and may, if observed, be so to you.

Remember that TIME is Money. He that can earn Ten Shillings a Day by his Labour, and goes abroad, or sits idle one half of that Day, tho' he spends but Sixpence during his Diversion or Idleness, ought not to reckon That the only Expence; he has really spent or rather thrown away Five Shillings besides.

Remember that CREDIT is Money. If a Man lets his Money lie in my Hands after it is due, he gives me the Interest, or so much as I can make of it during that Time. This amounts to a considerable Sum where a Man has good and large Credit, and makes good Use of it.

Remember that Money is of a prolific generating Nature. Money can beget Money, and its Offspring can beget more, and so on. Five Shillings turn'd, is Six: Turn'd again, 'tis Seven and Three Pence; and so on 'til it becomes an Hundred Pound. The more there is of it, the more it produces every Turning, so that the Profits rise quicker and quicker. He that kills a breeding Sow, destroys all her Offspring to the thousandth Generation. He that murders a Crown, destroys all it might have produc'd, even Scores of Pounds.

Remember that Six Pounds a Year is but a Groat a Day. For this little Sum (which may be daily wasted either in Time or Expence unperceiv'd) a Man of Credit may on his own Security have the constant Possession and Use of an Hundred Pounds. So much in Stock briskly turn'd by an industrious Man, produces great Advantage.

Remember this Saying, That the good Paymaster is Lord of another Man's Purse. He that is known to pay punctually and exactly to the Time he promises, may at any Time, and on any Occasion, raise all the Money his Friends can spare. This is sometimes of great Use: Therefore never keep borrow'd Money an Hour beyond the Time you promis'd, lest a Disappointment shuts up your Friend's Purse forever.

The most trifling Actions that affect a Man's Credit, are to be regarded. The Sound of your Hammer at Five in the Morning or Nine at Night, heard by a Creditor, makes him easy Six Months longer. But if he sees you at a Billiard Table, or hears your Voice in a Tavern, when you should be at Work, he sends for his Money the next Day. Finer Cloaths than he or his Wife wears, or greater Expence in any particular than he affords himself, shocks his Pride, and he duns you to humble you. Creditors are a kind of People, that have the sharpest Eyes and Ears, as well as the best Memories of any in the World.

Good-natur'd Creditors (and such one would always chuse to deal with if one could) feel Pain when they are oblig'd to ask for Money. Spare 'em that Pain, and they will love you. When you receive a Sum of Money, divide it among 'em in Proportion to your Debts. Don't be asham'd of paying a small Sum because you owe a greater. Money, more or less, is always welcome; and your Creditor had rather be at the Trouble of receiving Ten Pounds voluntarily brought him, tho' at ten different Times or Payments, than be oblig'd to go ten Times to demand it before he can receive it in a Lump. It shews, besides, that you are mindful of what you owe; it makes you appear a careful as well as an honest Man; and that still encreases your Credit.

Beware of thinking all your own that you possess, and of living accordingly. 'Tis a Mistake that many People who have Credit fall into. To prevent this, keep an exact Account for some Time of both your Expences and your Incomes. If you take the Pains at first to mention Particulars, it will have this good Effect; you will discover how wonderfully small trifling Expences mount up to large Sums, and will discern what might have been, and may for the future be saved, without occasioning any great Inconvenience.

In short, the Way of Wealth, if you desire it, is as plain as the Way to Market. It depends chiefly on two Words, INDUSTRY and FRUGALITY; i. e. Waste neither Time nor Money, but make the best Use of both. He that gets all he can honestly, and saves all he gets (necessary Expences excepted) will certainly become RICH; If that Being who governs the World, to whom all should look for a Blessing on their honest Endeavours, doth not in his wise Providence otherwise determine.

Benjamin Franklin (1706-90), born in Boston the son of a candle maker and soap boiler, began to work for his father at the age of ten. From age twelve to seventeen he was apprenticed to his half-brother James, who owned a printer's shop and to whose *New England Courant* he contributed his Dogood Papers. In 1723, the boy, who had little formal education but read widely, ran away to Philadelphia, where he worked in a printing shop. After his first stay in London, he returned to Philadelphia in 1726, built up his own press, began to issue *The Pennsylvania Gazette*, and soon established a successful business. He wrote on all kinds of subjects and earned great popularity through his *Poor Richard's Almanack* (1733-58). He became an influential leader in philanthropic, scientific and political affairs, initiated projects for paving, cleaning and lighting the streets, for a city police, and for the first circulating library, and founded the American Philosophical Society, a city hospital, and an Academy for the Education of Youth, which was the forerunner of the University of Pennsylvania. He invented the Franklin Stove and a new kind of clock and conducted his famous kite experiment to show that flashes of lightning were releases of electricity. In 1753 he was made deputy postmaster-general for the colonies, and in 1757 he was sent to England to secure better governmental conditions for the colonies. He remained abroad, with brief interruptions, until 1775, became acquainted with such thinkers as Burke, Hume, and Adam Smith, received honorary degrees from three British universities, and published important political and scientific papers. Convinced that Lord North was driving the colonies into rebellion, he returned to America, to serve in the Continental Congress, become postmaster-general, and aided in the drafting of the *Declaration of Independence*. Then he was sent to France, where he was celebrated as a witty sage from the backwoods and, in 1778, succeeded in securing a treaty to promote commerce and a defensive alliance. In 1783 he was a member of the commission that signed the Treaty of Paris, and two years later he returned home. There he became a member of the Federal Constitutional Convention and fought for the abolition of slavery. His *Autobiography*, which he had begun in 1771, was never finished and breaks off abruptly during the account of the year 1757. It was published in England, France and Germany before the American edition of 1818, and the complete work did not appear in English until 1867.

Vocabulary

4 shilling (n.): an amount of money in use in Britain and pre-revolution America equal to 12 (old) pence - **5 idle** (adj.): lazy, not working - **5 tho'** (conj.): old form of '(al)though' - **5 diversion** (n.): a turning aside from a course, activity, or use; s.th. that turns s.o.'s attention away from s.th. else that one does not wish to be noticed - **6 to reckon** (v.): to consider, to regard - **6 expence** (n.): old form of 'expense' - **10 prolific** (adj.): having or producing in large numbers - **10 to beget** (v.): (formal) to produce - **13 offspring** (n.): a child or children - **14 crown** (n.): a British coin worth 25 pence, used in former times as money but now made only on ceremonial occasions to be kept and not spent - **14 score** (n.): (often in combination) a group of 20 - **16 groat** (n.): (in England up to the middle of the 17th century and in pre-revolution America) a silver coin worth a few pence - **18 stock** (n.): a supply (of s.th.) for use - **18 brisk** (adj): quick and active - **22 to spare** (v.): to give up as not completely needed, afford to give - **23 lest** (conj.): (formal) in order that ... not, in case; for fear that - **24 trifling** (adj.): of slight importance or little value - **25 creditor** (n.): a person or firm to whom money is owed - **26 tavern** (n.): (old use) an inn; a small hotel or place where one can stay and/or drink alcohol, eat meals, etc. - **27 cloath** (n.): old form of 'clothes' - **28 to dun** (v.): to make persistent demands upon for payment - **28 to humble** (v.): to make (s.o. or o.s.) humble or lower in position - **30 to chuse** (v.): old form of 'to choose' - **35 lump** (n.): not divided into parts; altogether - **35 to shew** (v.): old form of 'to show' - **37 to encrease** (v.): old form of 'to increase' - **40 particulars** (n.): the facts (esp. about an event) - **42 to occasion** (v.): to cause - **45 frugality** (n.): the quality of not being wasteful, of being careful in the use of money, food, etc. - **48 endeavour** (n.): an effort, attempt - **48 providence** (n.): (an act or event showing) God's care or the kindness of fate.

Awareness

1 Write a short essay in which you state how and according to which criteria you organize your daily schedule with regard to work and leisure.

Comprehension

2 What reasons does Franklin provide for his statements that (a) time and (b) credit "is Money" (l. 4 and l. 7)?
3 What is Franklin's advice concerning the treatment of one's creditors?
4 What does one have to do in order to "certainly become rich" (l. 47)?
5 Sum up the major stages of Franklin's argument in your own words.

Analysis

6 Relate Franklin's "time is money" slogan to the general ideas of success and progress and consider the effects of this maxim upon the predominant life styles in capitalistic societies.
7 Assess the role which Franklin ascribes to work and investigate the degree to which an understanding of work as the central aspect of human existence is based on Biblical prescription.
8 Translate the message of *The Ladder of Success* into an essay in which you define what a young person who wants to become successful should (a) do and (b) avoid doing.
9 Define the version of "success" introduced in the cartoon on p. 48.

Opinion

10 Comment on Franklin's daily schedule from the *Autobiography* and compare it to your daily time table.
11 Consider, in the light of the concluding paragraph, the widespread notion that Franklin is a utilitarian for whom to appear virtuous is as good as to be virtuous.

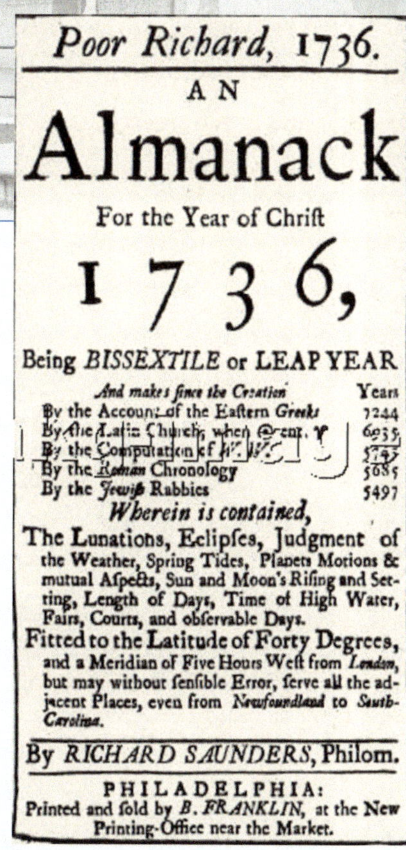

Poor Richard, 1736.

AN

Almanack

For the Year of Chriſt

1736,

Being *BISSEXTILE* or LEAP YEAR

And makes ſince the Creation	Years
By the Account of the Eaſtern *Greeks*	7244
By the Latin Church, when ☉ ent. ♈	6935
By the Computation of W. W.	5742
By the *Roman* Chronology	5685
By the *Jewiſh* Rabbies	5497

Wherein is contained,

The Lunations, Eclipſes, Judgment of the Weather, Spring Tides, Planets Motions & mutual Aſpects, Sun and Moon's Riſing and Setting, Length of Days, Time of High Water, Fairs, Courts, and obſervable Days.

Fitted to the Latitude of Forty Degrees, and a Meridian of Five Hours Weſt from *London*, but may without ſenſible Error, ſerve all the adjacent Places, even from *Newfoundland* to *South-Carolina*.

By *RICHARD SAUNDERS*, Philom.

PHILADELPHIA:
Printed and ſold by *B. FRANKLIN*, at the New Printing-Office near the Market.

Projects

12 Discuss Franklin's key concepts of "industry" and "frugality" in the light of Richard Weiss' observation that industry, frugality and prudence are "the great trinity of the Protestant [work] ethic."
13 Read Max Weber's seminal study "Die protestantische Ethik und der Geist des Kapitalismus" and discuss his evaluation of Franklin.
14 Compare the two German versions of "Advice" in Ferdinand Kürnberger's novel *Der Amerika-Müde* and in Weber's treatise with the original text and comment on the differences.

Internet Projects

15 Study the PBS website on Franklin (http://www.pbs.org/benfranklin/index.html) and the U.S. History website on "The Electric Ben Franklin" (http://www.ushistory.org/franklin/) and write an essay on Franklin's major discoveries and inventions.

13

Theodore Dreiser

"The Lobster and the Squid"*

In his trilogy *The Financier* (1912), *The Titan* (1914), and *The Stoic* (1947), Dreiser painted one of the most famous portraits of a big businessman in American literature. Dreiser's protagonist Frank Algernon Cowperwood develops the mentality which enables him to pursue his career at any price in a famous scene at the beginning of the first novel. – Theodore Dreiser, *The Financier* (London: Constable & Co., 1927), pp. 9-11.

"You realize, of course, it's not what you are that counts. It's who you know. Who do you know?"

Frank Cowperwood, even at ten, was a natural-born leader. At the day school he attended, and later at the Central High School, he was looked upon as one whose common sense could unquestionably be trusted in all cases. He was a sturdy youth, courageous and defiant. From the very start of his life, he wanted to know about economics and politics. He cared nothing for books. He was a clean, stocky, shapely boy, with a bright, clean-cut, incisive face; large, clear, grey eyes; a wide forehead; short, bristly, dark-brown hair. He had an incisive, quick-motioned, self-sufficient manner, and was forever asking questions with a keen desire for an intelligent reply. [...]

There was a fish-market not so very far from his home, and there, on his way to see his father at the bank, or conducting his brothers on after-school expeditions, he liked to look at a certain tank in front of one store where were kept odd specimens of sea-life [...] One day he saw a squid and a lobster put into the tank, and in connection with them was witness to a tragedy which stayed with him all his life and cleared things up considerably intellectually. The lobster, it appeared from the talk of the idle bystanders, was offered no food, as the squid was considered his rightful prey. He lay at the bottom of the clear glass tank on the yellow sand, apparently seeing nothing – you could not tell in which way his beady, black buttons of eyes were looking – but ap-parently they were never off the body of the squid. The latter, pale and waxy in texture, looking very much like pork fat or jade, moved about in torpedo fashion; but his movements were apparently never out of the eyes of his enemy, for by degrees small portions of his body began to disappear, snapped off by the relentless claws of his pursuer. The lobster would leap like a catapult to where the squid was apparently idly dreaming, and the squid, very alert, would dart away, shooting out at the same time a cloud of ink, behind which it would disappear. It was not always completely successful, however. Small portions of its body, or its tail were frequently left in the claws of the monster below. Fascinated by the drama, young Cowperwood came daily to watch.

One morning he stood in front of the tank, his nose almost pressed to the glass. Only a portion of the squid remained and his ink-bag was emptier than ever. In the corner of the tank sat the lobster, poised apparently for action.

The boy stayed as long as he could, the bitter struggle fascinating him. Now, maybe, or in an hour or a day, the squid might die, slain by the lobster, and the lobster would eat him. He looked again at the greenish-copperish engine of destruction in the corner and wondered when this would be. Tonight, maybe. He would come back tonight.

He returned that night, and lo! the expected had happened. There was a little crowd around the tank. The lobster was in the corner. Before him was the squid cut in two and partially devoured.

"He got him at last," observed one bystander. "I was standing right here an hour ago, and up he leaped and grabbed him. The squid was too tired. He wasn't quick enough. He did back up, but that lobster he calculated on his doing that. He's been figuring on his movements for a long time now. He got him today."

Frank only stared. Too bad he had missed this. The least touch of sorrow for the squid came to him as he stared at it slain. Then he gazed at the victor.

"That's the way it has to be, I guess," he commented to himself. "That squid wasn't quick enough." He figured it out. "The squid couldn't kill the lobster – he had no weapon. The lobster could kill the squid – he was heavily armed. There was nothing for the squid to feed on; the lobster had the squid as prey. What was the result to be? What else could it be? He didn't have a chance," he concluded finally, as he trotted on homeward.

The incident made a great impression on him. It answered in a rough way that riddle which had been annoying him so much in the past: "How is life organised?" Things lived on each other – that was it. Lobsters lived on squids and other things. What lived on lobsters? Men, of course! Sure, that was it! And what lived on men? he asked himself. Was it other men? Wild animals lived on men. And there were Indians and cannibals. And some men were killed by storms and accidents. He wasn't so sure about men living on men; but men did kill each other. How about wars and street fights and mobs? He had seen a mob once. It attacked the *Public Ledger* building as he was coming home from school. His father had explained why. It was about the slaves. That was it! Sure, men lived on men. Look at the slaves. They were men. That's what all this excitement was about these days. Men killing other men – negroes.

He went on home quite pleased with himself at his solution.

Vocabulary

Intro/3 to pursue (v.): to continue (steadily) with; to be busy with - **5 sturdy** (adj.): strong and firm, esp. in body - **5 defiant** (adj.): /dɪ'faɪənt/ showing no fear or respect; fearlessly refusing to obey - **8 stocky** (adj.): thick, short, and strong (in body) - **8 shapely** (adj.): having a body that has an attractive shape - **9 incisive** (adj.): /ɪn'saɪsɪv/ going directly to the center or main point of the matter that is being considered - **10 bristly** (adj.): like or full of short stiff coarse hair - **11 self-sufficient** (adj.): able to provide for one's needs without outside help - **12 keen** (adj.): (of the mind, the feelings, the senses, etc.) good, strong, quick at understanding - **18 squid** (n.): a sea creature of sizes from very large to very small with ten arms at one end of a long body strengthened by a feather-like shell inside - **18 lobster** (n.): a type of large eight-legged sea animal with a shell, the flesh of which may be eaten after boiling - **18 tank** (n.): a large container for storing liquid - **22 idle** (adj.): lazy, not working - **23 prey** (n.): an animal that is hunted and eaten by another animal - **26 beady** (adj.): (esp. of an eye) small, round, and shining, like a bead - **28 waxy** (adj.): /'wæksɪ/ (pale) like wax, that is, a solid material made of fats or oils and changing to a thick liquid when melted by heat - **28 texture** (n.): the degree of roughness or smoothness, coarseness or fineness, of a surface, esp. as felt by touch - **29 jade** (n.): /dʒeɪd/ a precious usually green stone from which ornaments and jewellery are made - **32 relentless** (adj.): without pity - **33 to leap** (v.): to act, pass, rise, etc., rapidly, as if with a jump - **35 alert** (adj.): watchful and ready to meet danger - **35 to dart away** (v.): to move suddenly and quickly away - **45 poised** (adj.): in a condition of (dangerous) uncertainty - **51 copperish** (adj.): having a copper (reddish-brown) color - **54 lo** (interj.): (old use) look - **57 to devour** (v.): to eat up quickly and hungrily - **61 to back up** (v.): to go backwards - **62 to figure on** (v.): (esp. AmE) to plan on, include in one's plans - **98 ledger** (n.): an account book recording the gains and money spent of a business, bank, etc.

Theodore Herman Albert Dreiser (1871-1945) was born in Terre Haute, Indiana, the ninth child of poor and fanatically religious German-speaking parents. They taught him to reject many human experiences as degrading, and he early developed a yearning for wealth and the kind of life which he later invented for his hero Cowperwood, the unscrupulous magnate of big business, who is the protagonist of the 'trilogy of desire' consisting of *The Financier* (1912), *The Titan* (1914), and *The Stoic* (1947). Having worked as a newspaper reporter in St. Louis, Chicago, Pittsburgh, and New York and having overcome his crass worship of success by studying Huxley and Spencer, Dreiser arrived at a view of life as a strangely magnificent but purposeless composite of warring energies. He temporarily interrupted his journalism to write *Sister Carrie* (1900), the story of a working girl and her life as the mistress of a man who descends the social ladder as she rises to success as an actress. Since the book was withheld from circulation because of its outspokenness, Dreiser had to earn his living by editing pulp magazines and women's fashion journals. His second novel, *Jenny Gerhardt* (1911) was again attacked for its candid depiction of American life, but it was with *An American Tragedy* (1925) that he finally won popular acclaim.

"I believe that life is a mess. [...] It is like yeast, a ferment, a thing that moves and may move for a minute, an hour, a year, or a hundred years, but that in the end will cease to move. The big eat the little that they may continue to move, the strong eat the weak that they may retain their strength. The lucky eat the most and move the longest, that is all." –

Captain Larsen in Jack London's *The Sea-Wolf (1904)*

Awareness

1 Collect, in class, what you know about Darwinism and Social Darwinism. Use Info Sheet 11.

Comprehension

2 What does young Cowperwood learn from the fight between the lobster and the squid?

3 Sum up what happens in the text in the form of a newspaper article.

Analysis

4 The fight between the lobster and the squid is a parable, that is a short allegorical story illustrating a moral or religious principle. Which principle does Cowperwood recognize as illustrated by the fight?

5 How can the cartoon about big fish eating little fish on page 49 be related to Dreiser's text?

6 Define the new variation of "Success" that is introduced in the other cartoon on page 48.

Project

7 Collect some material on the tenets of Social Darwinism, especially Herbert Spencer's famous maxim of 'the survival of the fittest,' and reassess Dreiser's text and the short excerpt from Jack London's *The Sea-Wolf* in this cultural context.

14

"Arnold Schwarzenegger: From Body Builder to Governor"*

Born in Graz, Austria, in 1947, Arnold Schwarzenegger emigrated to the U.S. in 1968 where he became the world's most successful body builder. In 1983 he attained U.S. citizenship. In the 80s he starred in action movies like *Conan the Barbarian* and *The Terminator* and by the 90s he was listed as one of the most successful Hollywood stars. Being a moderate Republican, Schwarzenegger was chosen by George Bush, Snr. as chairman of the President's Council on Physical Fitness and Sports. In 2003 he was elected Governor of California, and in 2006 he was re-elected. For 25 years Schwarzenegger was married to John F. Kennedy's niece Maria Shriver, but when, in 2011, it was revealed that he had fathered a son with one of his employees, the couple separated and Shriver filed for divorce. – In 1980 Studs Terkel published a collection of Interviews which includes the following statement by Arnold Schwarzenegger. – Studs Terkel, *American Dreams Lost and Found* (New York: Pantheon, 1980), pp. 129ff.

Call me Arnold.

I was born in a little Austrian town, outside Graz. It was a 300-year-old house.

When I was ten years old, I had the dream of being the best in the world in something. When I was fifteen, I had a dream that I wanted to be the best body builder in the world and the most muscular man. It was not only a dream I dreamed at night. It was also a daydream. It was so much in my mind that I felt it had to become a reality. It took me five years of hard work. Five years later, I turned this dream into reality and became Mr. Universe, the best-built man in the world.

"Winning" is a very important word. There is one that achieves what he wanted to achieve and there are hundreds of thousands that failed. It singles you out: the winner.

I came out second three times, but that is not what I call losing. The bottom line for me was: Arnold has to be the winner. I have to win more often the Mr. Universe title than anybody else. I won it five times consecutively. I hold the record as Mr. Olympia, the top professional body-building championship. I won it six times. That's why I retired. There was nobody even close to me. Everybody gave up competing against me. That's what I call a winner.

When I was a small boy, my dream was not to be big physically, but big in a way that everybody listens to me when I talk, that I'm a very important person, that people recognize me and see me as something special. I had a big need for being singled out.

Also my dream was to end up in America. When I was ten years old, I dreamed of being an American. At the time I didn't know much about America, just that it was a wonderful country. I felt it was where I belonged. I didn't like being in a little country like Austria. I did everything possible to get out. I did so in 1968, when I was twenty-one years old.

If I would believe in life after death, I would say my before-life I was living in America. That's why I feel so good here. It is the country where you can turn your dream into reality. Other countries don't have those things. When I came over here to America, I felt I was in heaven. In America, we don't have an obstacle. Nobody's holding you back.

Number One in America pretty much takes care of the rest of the world. You kind of run through the rest of the

world like nothing. I'm trying to make people in America aware that they should appreciate what they have here. You have the best tax advantages here and the best prices here and the best products here.

One of the things I always had was a business mind. When I was in high school, a majority of my classes were business classes. Economics and accounting and mathematics. When I came over here to this country, I really didn't speak English almost at all. I learned English and then started taking business courses, because that's what America is best known for: business. Turning one dollar into a million dollars in a short period of time. Also when you make money, how do you keep it?

That's one of the most important things when you have money in your hand, how can you keep it? Real estate is one of the best ways of doing that. I own apartment buildings, office buildings, and raw land. That's my love, real estate.

I have emotions. But what you do, you keep them cold or you store them away for a time. You must control your emotions, you must have command over yourself. Three, four months before a competition, I could not be interfered by other people's problems. This is sometimes called selfish. It's the only way you can be if you want to achieve something. Any emotional things inside me, I try to keep cold so it doesn't interfere with my training.

Many times things really touched me. I felt them and I felt sensitive about them. But I had to talk myself out of it. I had to suppress those feelings in order to go on. Sport is one of those activities where you really have to concentrate. You must pay attention a hundred percent to the particular thing you're doing. There must be nothing else on your mind. Emotions must not interfere. Otherwise, you're thinking about your girlfriend. You're in love, your positive energies get channelled into another direction rather than going into our weight room or making money.

You have to choose at a very early date what you want: a normal life or to achieve things you want to achieve. I never wanted to win a popularity contest in doing things the way people want me to do it. I went the road I thought was best for me. A few people thought I was cold, selfish. Later they found out that's not the case. After I achieve my goal, I can be Mr. Nice Guy. You know what I mean?

California is to me a dreamland. It is the absolute combination of everything I was always looking for. It has all the money in the world there, show business there, wonderful weather there, beautiful country, ocean is there. Snow skiing in the winter, you can go in the desert the same day. You have beautiful-looking people there. They all have a tan.

I believe very strongly in the philosophy of staying hungry. If you have a dream and it becomes a reality, don't stay satisfied with it too long. Make up a new dream and hunt after that one and turn it into reality. When you have that dream achieve, make up a new dream.

I am a strong believer in Western philosophy, the philosophy of success, of progress, of getting rich. The Eastern philosophy is passive, which I believe in maybe three percent of the times, and the ninety-seven percent is Western, conquering and going on. It's a beautiful philosophy, and America should keep it up.

Arnold Schwarzenegger's Acceptance Speech

[...]

I want to [...] thank the people of California. From the time I came over to this country, you've opened up your arms to me. You've received me. You've given me opportunities, endless amount of opportunities. Everything that I have is because of California. I came over — that's right. I came here with absolutely nothing. And California has given me absolutely everything. And today, and today, California has given me the greatest gift of all. You've given me your trust by voting for me.

Thank you very much to all the people of California for giving me their great trust [...]

Gov. Arnold Schwarzenegger's inaugural address

To the thousands of you who came here today, I took this oath to serve you. To others all across this state – Democrats, Republicans, Independents – it makes no difference. I took this oath to serve you. To those who have no power, to those who have dropped out – too weary or disappointed with politics as usual – I took the oath to serve you. I say to everyone here today and to all Californians, I will not forget my oath and I will not forget you. (...)

But for guidance, let's look back in history to a period I studied when I became a citizen. The summer of 1787. Delegates of the original 13 states were meeting in Philadelphia.

The dream of a new nation was falling apart. Events were spiraling downward. Divisions were deep. Merchant against farmer. Big states against small. North against South.

Our founding fathers knew that the fate of the union was in their hands, just as the fate of California is in our hands.

What happened in that summer of 1787 is that they put their differences aside – and produced the blueprint for our government; our Constitution. Their coming together has been called "the Miracle of Philadelphia." Now, the members of the Legislation and I must bring about the "Miracle of Sacramento" – a miracle based on cooperation, good will, new ideas – and devotion to the long-term good of California.

When we face may look insurmountable. But I learned something from all those years of training and competing. What I learned is that we are always stronger than we know. And California is like that, too.

We are stronger than we know. (...)

Ladies and gentlemen, I have an immigrant's optimism that what I have learned in citizen class is true: The system does work.

And I believe that with all of my heart.

I have big hopes for California. President Reagan spoke of America as "the shining city on the hill." I see California as the golden dream by the sea.

Perhaps some think this is fanciful or poetic, but to an immigrant like me, who, as a boy, saw Soviet tanks rolling through the streets of Austria, to someone like me who came here with absolutely nothing and gained absolutely everything, it is not fanciful to see this state as a golden dream.

For millions of people around the world, California has always glimmered with hope and glowed with opportunity. Millions of people around the world send their dreams to California with the hope their lives will follow.

My fellow citizens.

I have taken the oath to uphold the Constitution of California. Now, with your help and God's, I will also uphold the dream that is California.

Vocabulary

18 bottom line (n.): used to tell s.o. what is the most important part of a situation or the most important thing to consider - **43 obstacle** (n.): s.th. that makes it difficult to achieve s.th. – **48 to appreciate** (v.): to understand how good or useful s.o. or s.th. is - **53 accounting** (n.): the profession or work of keeping or checking financial accounts, calculating taxes, etc. - **61 real estate** (n.): the business of selling houses or land - **69 to interfere** (v.): to deliberately get involved in a situation where you are not wanted or needed - **81 to channel** (v.): to control s.th. such as money or energy towards a particular purpose.

Explanations

11 Mr. Universe: a body building title - **21 Mr. Olympia**: another body building title - **63 raw land**: a piece of land without any buildings on it - **82 weight room**: room in which you lift weights for fitness or body building - **93 Mr. Nice Guy** – s.o. who behaves honestly and fairly.

Awareness

1 What is the 'Western Philosophy' Schwarzenegger talks about in the first text?

Comprehension

2 Explain the term 'California as the golden dream by the sea'.
3 Find and name the differences in the two texts regarding Schwarzenegger's image of the 'American Dream'.

Opinion

4 Collect your images of California. Do you think that California stands out in terms of its possibilities to fulfil the 'American Dream'? See text 3, project 10.
5 Do you see Schwarzenegger's career as an example of an American Dream realized?

Internet Project

6 Use the relevant internet sites to gather information about (a) the movies Schwarzenegger starred in and (b) the stages of his political career. Compare the roles he played in his films to his 'real life'-career, and discuss possible connections.

15 The American Dream of Owning a House

In his book *The American Dream: A Short History of an Idea That Shaped a Nation* (2003), Jim Cullen has a chapter on "Detached Houses: The Dream of Home Ownership," in which he states:
"No American Dream has broader appeal, and no American Dream has been quite so widely realized. Roughly two-thirds of Americans owned their homes at the start of this century, and it seems reasonable to believe that many of the remaining third will go on to do so. And if, like other American Dreams, this one is imperfect, even fatally flawed, it is also extraordinarily resilient and versatile."

In June 2002, President Bush celebrated National Homeownership Month and declared that he would sign into law the "American Dream Downpayment Assistance Act" (ADDI), aimed at helping about 40,000 families a year with their down payment and thus meant to further strengthen America's housing market. He said:

"You know, I mentioned the word American Dream in Atlanta. I also recognize that some people aren't sure that dream extends to them. Some people don't even know what the dream means. And our job – our jobs, our collective jobs, is to make sure that notion of the American Dream extends into every single neighborhood around this country. [...] I believe owning something is a part of the American Dream, as well. I believe when somebody owns their own home, they're realizing the American Dream."

But when in 2007 the Subprime Mortgage Crisis hit, an ever increasing number of home owners could no longer pay their rates and lost their houses in a huge wave of mortgage delinquencies and foreclosures. Many of them who were evicted from their houses formed a nation-wide self-help group, and once more the connection between the American Dream and owning a house of one's own became obvious when they decided to call their organization "Save the American Dream."

(For further details and the full text of two relevant speeches by President Bush see Info Sheet 12.)

Comprehension

1 Use Info Sheet 12 to learn about subprime mortgages, 'foreclosure,' 'eviction,' etc.

Analysis

2 Translate the message of the cartoon into a descriptive text.

Opinion

3 Why is owning a house of one's own such a central ingredient of the American Dream?
4 Some say that the effects of the subprime mortgage crisis have put an end to the American Dream. Comment.

Project

5 Use the internet to research the subprime mortgage crisis and its effect upon the worldwide crisis of the financial markets.
6 Use the slides of selected "American Dream Houses" from Scotty's Castle in Death Valley to Elvis Presley's Graceland in Memphis on the CD and deal with the tasks provided there.

16

Paul Harris

"Wake Up: the American Dream Is Over"

On 8 June 2006, Paul Harris published an article in the British Sunday paper *The Observer*, in which he argued that the growing gap between the rich and the poor in the U.S. has made it impossible for the latter to achieve the American Dream. The excerpt is taken from http://www.guardian.co.uk/world/2006/jun/08/usa.comment.

There is a common response to America among foreign writers: the USA is a land of extremes where the best of things are just as easily found as the worst.

This is a cliché. But it is often hard to argue with when surveying America's political and cultural landscape. America has some of the worst urban sprawl in the world and also the most beautiful and well-protected wildernesses. Its politics is awash with lobbyist inspired corruption. Yet passionate political engagement among millions of Americans puts many other countries to shame. [...]

So in this land of black and white, we should not be too surprised to find some of the biggest gaps between rich and poor in the world. Such a yawning chasm is just the American Way, it would seem. Besides, the American Dream offers a way out to everyone. All someone has to do is work hard and climb the ladder towards the top. No class system or government stands in the way.

Sadly, this old argument is no longer true. Over the past few decades there has been a fundamental shift in the structure of the American economy. The gap between rich and poor has widened and widened. As it does so, the ability to cross that gap gets smaller and smaller. This is far from business as usual but there seems little chance of it stopping, not least because it appears to be government policy.

Over the past 25 years the median US family income has gone up 18 percent. For the top one percent, however, it has gone up 200 percent. A quarter of a century ago the top fifth of Americans had an average income 6.7 times that of the bottom fifth. Now it is 9.8 times.

Inequalities have grown worse in different regions. In California, home to both Beverly Hills and the gang-ridden slums of Compton, incomes for lower class families have fallen by four percent since 1969. For upper class families they have risen 41 percent.

This has led to an economy hugely warped in favour of a small slice of very rich Americans. The wealthiest one percent of households now control a third of the national wealth. The wealthiest 10 percent control two-thirds of it. This is a society that is splitting down the middle and it has taken place against a backdrop of economic growth.

Between 1980 and 2004 America's GDP went up by almost two-thirds. But instead of making everyone better off, it has made only a part of the country wealthier, as another part slips ever more into the black hole of the working poor. There are now 37 million Americans living in poverty, and at 12.7 percent of the population, it is the highest percentage in the developed world.

Yet the tax burden on America's rich is falling, not growing. The top 0.01 percent of households has seen their tax bite fall by a full 25 percentage points since 1980. That was when 'trickle down' economics began, arguing that the rich spending more would benefit everyone as a whole. But America's poor have simply been getting poorer: clearly that theory has not worked in reality.

And still the American government is set on tax breaks for the rich. [...] The effect of all this has been to scotch that long-cherished notion of the American Dream: that honest toil is enough to reap the rewards and let even the poorest join the middle class, or maybe even strike it rich. A survey last year showed that such economic mobility (a measure of those people trying to make the Dream come true) was lower in America than Canada, Germany, Norway, Denmark, Sweden and Finland. In fact, the only country doing as bad as America was Britain.

Now this is not some argument against capitalism. Inequality is inevitable. It is a good thing. People need incentives. People need competition. People need markets. Some people will always be poor. Others deserve to be rich. But at the moment it looks like the rules of the game are being fixed in America in favour of the wealthy. The gap between rich and poor will only get wider. That is very dangerous.

Don't just take my word for it. Take Buffet's. After all he doesn't have anything to gain from criticising current policy. In fact he has hundreds of millions of dollars to lose. "If class warfare is being waged in America," he has written, "my class is clearly winning." When even the rich are starting to think they are getting too many tax cuts, then you know something has gone very wrong.

The 2010 Legatum Prosperity Index

This global assessment of wealth and well-being (http://www.prosperity.com/) which bases its rankings upon the factors that drive economic growth and produce happy citizens, ranks the U.S. as No. 10 (Norway as No. 1, Germany as No. 15). Here are some details about the U.S.:

Economy	**14th**
confidence in financial institutions	86th
domestic savings rate	84th
Entrepreneurship and Opportunity	**3rd**
optimism about job availability	86th
...perception that working hard gets you ahead	28th
Governance	**4th**
preservation of the environment	33rd
public confidence in the military	11th
Education	**9th**
primary level education	68th
secondary level education	39th
tertiary level education	6th
public satisfaction with education	57th
Health	**1st**
life expectancy	27th
adequate food and shelter	31st
satisfaction with standard of living	28th
Safety and Security	**25th**

Vocabulary

6 urban sprawl (n.): the spread of city buildings and houses into an area that used to be countryside, or the area in which this has happened – **8 awash (with)** (adj.): containing too many things or people of a particular kind – **14 chasm** (n.): here a big difference between two groups – **37 warped** (adj.): bent or twisted so that it is not the correct shape – **59 to scotch** (v.): to stop s.th. from happening by firmly doing s.th. to prevent it – **70 incentive** (n.): s.th. that encourages you to work harder, start a new activity, etc.

Explanations

33 Beverly Hills: a city in Los Angeles County, CA, which is entirely surrounded by the city of Los Angeles. Among its 34,000 inhabitants are Hollywood celebrities, corporate executives and other wealthy people, making it one of the most affluent cities in the world. – **34 Compton**: a city in southern Los Angeles County with a population of about 100,000. It was notorious for gang violence as caused by the Bloods, the Crips and the Sueños, and in the late 80s its violent reputation was popularized by such gangsta rap groups as Compton's Most Wanted and N.W.A. – **43 GDP**: short for gross domestic product, the market value of all goods and services produced in a country in a given period – **53 'trickle down' economics**: the policy of providing across the board tax cuts or benefits to businesses, in the belief that this will indirectly benefit the broad population. Its proponents argue that economic growth flows down from the top to the bottom, thus indirectly benefiting also those who do not directly benefit from the policy changes. – **76 Warren Buffet**: (*1930) an American investor, industrialist, and philanthropist. He is regarded as one of the most successful investors in the world and was ranked as the world's wealthiest person in 2008.

Comprehension

1 How does Harris define the American Dream?

Analysis

2 Retrace the steps in Harris' argument about why "the American Dream is over."
3 Compare what Harris says about the American taxation system with the situation in Germany.

Opinion

4 Do you agree that the widening "gap between rich and poor" makes it impossible for the latter to achieve their American Dream?

Project

5 Have a debate, with one party basing its arguments on Fareed Zakaria, "Are America's Best Days Behind Us?" and the other on David von Drehle, "Don't Bet Against the United States," both in *Time*, 14 March 2011, with the cover captions "Yes, America Is in Decline" and "No, America Is Still No. 1."

17 The Sierra Club

"Driving up the Heat: SUVs and Global Warming"

The Sierra Club is the oldest environmentalist group in the U.S. Founded by John Muir in 1892, it has been responsible for the creation of several National Parks and is still an important part of the environmentalist movement. Today, the Sierra Club supports an environmentally conscious way of life. – http://www.sierraclub.org/globalwarming/SUVreport.

Switching from driving an average car to a 13mpg SUV for one year would waste more energy than if you...

- Left your refrigerator door open for 6 years
- Left your bathroom light burning for 30 years or
- Left your color television turned on for 28 years

Background

When it comes to wasting energy, SUVs are unrivaled. Built with outdated, gas-guzzling technology, many SUVs get just 13 miles per gallon. And the higher gas prices are, the more money they waste.

Auto-industry advertising portrays SUVs as the ticket to freedom and the great outdoors. Commercials depict them climbing massive snow-capped mountains or tearing through desert sand dunes, taking their owners into the wild. In reality, the only off-road action many of these vehicles see is accidentally driving through a flower bed next to the driveway.

Missing from these ads are other contributions from SUVs – the brown haze of air pollution hanging over many of our national parks, images of weather disasters linked to global warming or the oil derricks and tankers needed to feed gas-guzzling SUVs. In contrast to Detroit's carefully crafted image, SUVs have a dark side. They spew out 43 percent more global-warming pollution and 47 percent more air pollution than an average car. SUVs are four times more likely than cars to roll over in an accident and three times more likely to kill the occupants in a rollover. They also cost the owner thousands more on gasoline.

Worsening the Threat of Global Warming

Because the government classifies SUVs as "light trucks" rather than cars, SUVs have a license to guzzle more gas and pollute more than cars. In 1975, when fuel-economy standards were first adopted, "light truck" referred to a vehicle used to haul hay on the farm or gravel at a construction site. At that time, light trucks comprised only 20 percent of the vehicle market. Today, SUVs, mini-vans and other light trucks make up nearly half of new vehicles sold. They are far more likely to haul lattés home from Starbucks than lumber from the yard. Even though Detroit has technology that could make them both cleaner and safer, SUVs and other light trucks are still held to low environmental standards, roll over more than cars and pose greater danger to other vehicles than cars do.

The world's leading climate scientists have warned that there is now 30 percent more carbon dioxide – the primary global-warming gas – in the atmosphere than a century ago. The burning of fossil fuels is the primary source of this CO_2 pollution. Over the same period of

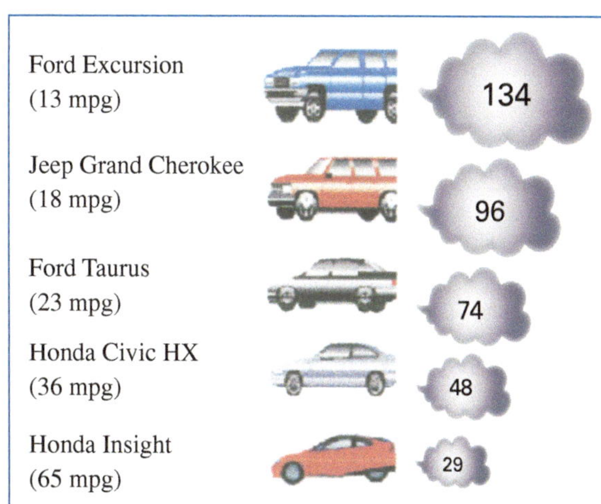

time, the average surface temperature of the earth has risen more than 1 degree Fahrenheit.

Due to these changes, we are already seeing signs of global warming. The 1990s was the hottest decade on record and the 11 hottest years on record have all occurred in the past 13 years.

Extreme drought conditions and changing rainfall patterns have occurred across the country, setting the stage for wildfires, which decimated areas from Florida to California. Record heat waves have killed hundreds in Chicago and infectious-disease outbreaks linked to global warming have sickened or killed hundreds from Texas to New York, shut down Disney World and re-introduced Americans to dengue fever, malaria and encephalitis. Sea levels have risen between four and 10 inches and glacial ice is rapidly retreating on five continents.

The world's leading scientists warn that over the 21st century, CO_2 levels are expected to double, raising sea levels two feet or more, worsening smog and leaving our children to cope with a more hostile climate.

America's cars and light trucks alone produce nearly 20 percent of U.S. CO_2 pollution. That's more than all but four countries worldwide! And transportation is the fastest-growing sector of global-warming pollution in the nation. Popular light trucks pump out 237 million tons of global-warming pollution into our atmosphere each year. That's because every gallon of gas burned emits 28 pounds of CO_2 into the atmosphere.

SUVs Emit More Air Pollution Than Cars

Nearly 117 million Americans live in areas where the air is unhealthy to breathe, according to the American Lung Association. Light trucks, which can spew up to three times more smog-forming pollution than cars, magnify this growing health threat. The increased air pollution can lead to more asthma, bronchitis and other health problems.

U.S. autos emit more CO_2 than all but four countries.

Top 5 Global-Warming Polluters:

1. United States 2. China 3. Russia 4. Japan 5. U.S. Cars

Air pollution is not exclusively an urban problem. National parks from Maine's Acadia to Virginia's Shenandoah and North Carolina's Great Smokey Mountains all have severe air-pollution problems that match major metropolitan areas. Pollution monitors are now installed at some trailheads in Mt. Rainier National Park to warn hikers when smog reaches unsafe levels.

The U.S. Environmental Protection Agency adopted new "Tier 2" tailpipe pollution standards in 1999 to cut smog (but not CO_2) from cars and SUVs. However, these rules will not go into effect until 2004 and the auto industry has until 2009 to clean up its largest SUVs.

The More You Guzzle, The More You Pollute

Represented on p. 57 is the total tonnage of CO_2 produced by SUVs and other vehicles over a 124,000-mile lifetime.

Analysis

1 Why is, according to the cartoon on page 57, an attempt to save fuel "distinctly un-American"?
2 Explain the meaning of the cartoon printed above.

Opinion

3 Do you think that SUVs are reasonable vehicles?

Project

4 Gather information about SUVs in general. Use the websites of car manufacturers and check whether the figures given for specific cars on page 57 have meanwhile been improved.
5 Make a list of means of reducing the CO_2 emission of cars (from smaller engines to speed limits) and discuss their effects.

Vocabulary

title: SUV: short for **sports utility vehicle**, a type of vehicle that is bigger than a car and is made for traveling over rough ground - **1 mpg**: miles per gallon, used to describe the amount of petrol used by a car - **8 to guzzle** (v.): to eat or drink a lot of s.th., eagerly and quickly, showing disapproval. If a vehicle guzzles petrol, it uses a lot of it in a wasteful way. - **19 haze** (n.): smoke, dust, or mist in the air which is difficult to see through - **21 derrick** (n.): a tall tower built over an oil well, used to raise and lower the drill - **24 to spew out** (phr. v.): to flow out of s.th. quickly in large quantities, or to make s.th. flow out in this way - **28 occupant** (n.): s.o. who is in a room, vehicle, etc. at a particular time - **35 to haul** (v.): to pull s.th. heavy with a continuous steady movement - **36 gravel** (n.): small stones, used to make a surface for paths, roads, etc. - **40 lumber** (n.): pieces of wood used for building that have been cut to specific lengths and widths - **49 fossil fuel** (n.): a fuel such as coal or oil that is produced by the very gradual decaying of animals or plants over millions of years - **65 glacial** (adj.): relating to ice and glaciers, or formed by glaciers - **78 to emit** (v.): to send out gas, heat, light, sound, etc. - **96 trailhead** (n.): the starting point of a hiking trail - **100 tailpipe** (n.): a pipe on a vehicle or machine through which gas or steam passes

18

Valdis Wish

"USA: Rethinking the American Dream"

On 3 June 2010 on the Allianz Knowledge Site, Valdis Wish published this article about the all too often overlooked effects which the pursuit of the American Dream has upon the increase of global warming (http://knowledge.allianz.com/climate/country_profiles/?132/climate-profile-us-intro).

The United States is a climate paradox. It is the second biggest emitter of CO_2, but the country boasts some of the most active scientists, organizations, and politicians fighting global warming.

The United States produces around a quarter of the world's carbon dioxide emissions making it the world's second biggest emitter of CO_2 after China. The problem is, the U.S. represents less than five percent of the world's population. U.S. leaders argue in its defense that the economic power of the country represents 25 percent of global economic output.

Energy Consumption

The United States has long been a very large consumer of energy. Figures from the World Wide Fund for Nature (WWF) show that the average American is responsible for 24 tons of carbon dioxide emissions per year, compared to 11 tons in the United Kingdom and France, 5 tons in Brazil, and 2 tons in India.

America's massive carbon footprint is due to its sheer size and economic success. Over the last 25 years, the United States has enjoyed the largest annual economic and population growth rate of any mature industrial economy in the world.

Americans use a lot of energy to run their many electronic appliances, and to heat or cool buildings, particularly during the very hot summers and cold winters that affect much of the continent. Americans also drive a lot, owing to their country's size and relatively cheap gasoline. Retail prices for gas are less than half the level in Germany or the United Kingdom. Most American families have at least two vehicles.

In the search for good schools and safe environments, many Americans have moved away from city centres thereby extending the boundaries of suburbia. With little or no investment in public transportation, distances travelled and therefore gas usage have increased hugely during the late 20th century.

Climate Politics

For years the world's biggest economy was reluctant to take steps to reduce its carbon footprint. Of 53 countries surveyed by Germanwatch, only two countries scored worse than the United States in terms of emissions trends and climate policy. While most other industrialized nations have agreed to the reductions in CO_2 emissions mandated by the Kyoto Protocol, the U.S. has rejected the treaty.

Because of strong opposition from both the Democratic and Republican parties, the treaty was never ratified by the U. S. Senate. President Barack Obama has now promised to revive stalling negotiations on a follow-up treaty to the Kyoto Protocol. Still, a number of U.S. politicians are opposed to mandatory emissions caps, saying it would retard economic growth and lead to higher unemployment.

Instead of the Kyoto Protocol, political leaders in Washington have tended to prefer non-binding, voluntary measures aimed at improving efficiency and promoting technological solutions – a policy that environmentalists say has so far been ineffective, because the country's emissions continue to increase.

But the tune in Washington is changing. Public awareness about the risks of global warming is growing, and local policy initiatives to reduce emissions have proven politically popular in states like California. However, the ongoing economic crisis that has hit the U.S. particularly hard might dilute radical steps to address global warming.

Anticipating future policies and increasing consumer demand for energy efficient products, U.S. companies may actually be ahead of their government. They are already investing billions of dollars to develop new products and services. When oil prices reached record-highs, foreign and domestic auto manufacturers started to see increasing demand for more fuel-efficient cars in the U.S. market.

As in China and Europe, the renewable energy and biofuels sectors in the United States are growing rapidly. According to the Worldwatch Institute, around 10,000 U.S. businesses and 110,000 households are now using certified "green" electricity generated from renewable resources.

The USA is no longer the number one climate culprit, but President Obama's ambitious climate change agenda has collapsed under political and economic pressure. What will America's climate future look like?

Vocabulary

34 suburbia (n.): suburbs in general, and the behavior, opinions, and ways of living that are typical of people who live there; often used to show disapproval - **50 to stall** (v.): inform. to deliberately delay because you are not ready to do s.th. - **52 emission cap** (n.): an upper limit that is put on the amount of emission - **67 to dilute** (v.): to make a quality, belief, etc. weaker or less effective - **83 culprit** (n.): the person who is guilty of a crime or doing s.th. wrong

Explanations

14 World Wide Fund for Nature: formerly named the **World Wildlife Fund**, which remains its official name in Canada and the U.S., the WWF is the world's largest independent conservation organization with over 5 million supporters, working in more than 90 countries and supporting around 1,300 conservation and environmental projects around the world. - **41 Germanwatch**: a non-profit NGO founded in 1991 and based in Bonn, which seeks to influence public policy with regard to trade, the environment, and relations between industrialized northern and underdeveloped southern countries - **45 Kyoto Protocol**: a protocol to the UN Framework Convention on Climate Change (UNFCCC), aimed at fighting global warming. It was adopted in December 1997 in Kyoto, Japan, and by July 2010, 191 states had signed and ratified it. The UNFCCC is an international environmental treaty aiming at "stabilization of greenhouse gas concentrations in the atmosphere at a level that would prevent dangerous anthropocentric interference with the climate system." - **79 Worldwatch Institute**: a globally focused environmental research organization based in Washington, D.C., which helps to inform politicians and the public about the links between the world economy and its environmental support systems.

Comprehension

1 Why do Americans use such a lot of energy?
2 What was the Kyoto Protocol? Find out why the U.S. chose not to sign it.

Analysis

3 Explain the concept of the "carbon footprint."
4 What are the connections between the American Dream and the consumption of energy?

Opinion

5 What can you and your family household do to save energy?
6 An ancient proverb states "We have not inherited the earth from our ancestors, we have only borrowed it from our children." Comment.

Project

7 Use the internet to research what has happened since Kyoto (the *Bali Road Map* of 2007, the *Copenhagen Summit* of 2009, etc.).

19 New American Dream

The organization "New American Dream" (http://www.newdream.org/) was founded in 1997 to address the environmental and social impacts of unsustainable consumption. Meanwhile the group has built a "New Dream Community" of more than 140,000 Americans who embrace less materialistic lifestyles and make healthier choices, and it has reached millions of Americans through its media campaigns and shifted billions of dollars into environmentally superior goods through its Responsible Purchasing Network. The organization has this to say about its vision of a 'new' American Dream:

A Vision of a New American Dream

For generations of Americans, the American dream stood for opportunity. The dream was rooted in the belief that, in a peaceful and democratic society, citizens were free to pursue their goals, and honest effort would result in a satisfactory degree of material comfort. The idealistic notion that in America one might reasonably aspire to a better life for oneself and one's family was a powerful symbol. It spoke not merely to personal aspirations but to our aim as a society as well.

Unfortunately, in recent decades the traditional American dream has been displaced by a "more is better" focus that promotes not quality of life, but rather the unbridled production and consumption of stuff. While this simplified version of the dream succeeded in boosting the US economy – now the biggest in the world in terms of material production and consumption – it has failed in more important ways. According to studies, all this material wealth isn't making us any happier than we were before the boom. Worse yet, shifting the prize from well-being to acquisition actually endangers some of the very things we cherish. The "more is better" dream is unsustainable personally, as it draws American families into a work-and-spend treadmill that depletes savings and clutters lives. It is unsustainable environmentally, as it fuels a level of resource consumption that the planet cannot keep up with. The "more is better" dream, in fact, is denying our children their fair opportunity for comfort, security and a healthy environment.

The Center for a New American Dream envisions a society that values more of what matters – not just "more." New American Dream is dedicated to helping support and nurture an American dream that revives the spirit of the traditional dream – but with a new emphasis on non-material values like financial security, fairness, community, health, time, nature, and fun. We see both a nation and a world in which a healthy global ecosystem anchors a just society offering all citizens the freedom, the resources and the personal security necessary to pursue their dreams, connect with the natural world, and enjoy a high quality of life. Some key elements of this new American dream are as follows:

A Higher Quality of Life

We envision a society in which citizens are able to meet material needs and pursue their dreams; where there is broad recognition that quality of life includes not just material wealth but also non-material values, relationships, and experiences; where there is more time for families, leisure, community service; where progress is measured not simply by changes in gross domestic product, but rather by indicators that more truly reflect improvements to quality of life, environmental sustainability, and social and economic fairness.

A Healthy Environment

We envision a society whose ecological footprint is in step with Earth's capacity, so that we are living in balance with what the natural world has to offer and we protect the resource base for future generations. Everyone should have access to clean air, clean water, healthy food, and adequate resources.

More Fairness

We envision a world that works for all; a world in which everyone has the opportunity to achieve a high quality of life; a world in which wealthy nations and individuals do not overconsume natural resources while the poor do without; a world in which workers at all parts of the supply chain are provided with safe working conditions and just compensation; a world where no one is denied access to basic needs such as food, clothing, shelter, health care, education, safety; a world where citizen influence over government policies is elevated over moneyed influence.

Strong Communities

We envision strong, tightly woven, participatory communities; more direct relationships between local producers and consumers; livable, walkable neighborhoods connected via accessible and affordable transportation systems with natural areas, parks, and open spaces available to all.

Healthy Economy and Marketplace

We envision a vibrant economy that operates in deference to both citizen needs and ecological limits; where advertising informs rather than manipulates, overwhelms, and preys upon insecurities; where citizens can choose not to receive commercial messages and no advertising is targeted at young children; where energy production and industrial processes do not exacerbate climate change nor degrade important biological communities; where materials are continuously recycled back into the manufacturing process and nothing is wasted; where environmentally and socially preferable products are widely available and competitively priced; where consumers have easy access to information that allows them to make informed choices – information about the economic, environmental, and social impacts associated with the entire life cycle of available products.

Vocabulary

11 aspiration (n. usu. pl.): a strong desire to have or achieve s.th. - **17 unbridled** (adj.): lit. not controlled and too extreme or violent - **20 to boost** (v.): to increase or improve s.th. and make it more successful - **29 unsustainable** (adj.): unable to continue at the same rate or in the same way - **31 treadmill** (n.): work or a way of life that seems very boring because you always have to do the same things - **31 to deplete** (v.): to reduce the amount of s.th. that is present or available - **37 to envision** (v.): to imagine s.th. that you think might happen in the future, esp. s.th. that you think will be good - **87 participatory** (adj.): *form.* involving everyone who will be affected - **94 vibrant** (adj.): full of activity or energy in a way that is exciting and attractive - **95 deference** (n.): *form.* polite behavior that shows that you respect s.o. and are therefore willing to accept their opinions or judgment - **100 to exacerbate** (v.): to make a bad situation worse

Comprehension

1 What is "sustainability"?

2 What is the meaning of the "New American Dream," and what are the problems associated with a "more is better" philosophy?

Analysis

3 Make a list of the major aims of the "New American Dream" organization and characterize each of these aims.

Opinion

4 Discuss the vision of a society governed by the "New American Dream." Explain whether you would/would not like to live in such a society.

Project

5 Download the New American Dream Wallet Buddy (http://www.newdream.org/walletbuddy.pdf), cut it out, put it together, give it to a friend, and convince him or her why they should carry their credit card in this buddy.

20 Casting Crowns

"American Dream"

In 1999, youth pastor Mark Hall (now a songwriter and the lead vocalist) started a Christian rock band at First Baptist Church in downtown Daytona Beach, Florida, as a student worship band. The group grew, and in 2001 relocated to Stockbridge, Georgia. More members joined, and they called themselves Casting Crowns. In 2003, the band released its debut album *Casting Crowns* with the lyrics of all songs but one being based on verses from the Bible. Two years later, this album was certified Platinum with over 1,000,000 copies sold in the U.S., and Casting Crowns became one of the fastest selling bands in Christian-music history. Meanwhile they have won Grammy and Dove Awards. Four of its members still minister at Eagle's Landing First Baptist Church in McDonough, Georgia, and its frontman Mark Hall calls its music a "ministry of discipleship."

On their 2003 album the group has the song "American Dream," which is a critique of the frightful consequences of "chasing the American dream" as wrongly understood in a merely materialist sense, and a plea for replacing the rat race for money and material possessions with such values as marital and parental love and family togetherness and for the overdue redefinition of the Dream in the context of Christian virtues.

"American Dream"

All work no play may have made Jack a dull boy
But all work no God has left Jack with a lost soul
But he's moving on full steam
He's chasing the American dream
And he's gonna give his family finer things

"Not this time son I've no time to waste
Maybe tomorrow we'll have time to play"
And then he slips into his new BMW
And drives farther and farther and farther away

Cause he works all day and tries to sleep at night
He says things will get better;
Better in time
[Chorus]

So he works and he builds with his own two hands
And he pours all he has in a castle made with sand
But the wind and the rain are comin' crashing in
Time will tell just how long his kingdom stands
His kingdom stands

Well his American Dream is beginning to seem
More and more like a nightmare
With every passing day
"Daddy, can you come to my game?"
"Oh Baby, please don't work late."
Another wasted weekend
And they are slipping away

'Cause he works all day and lies awake at night
He tells them things are getting better
Just take a little more time
[Chorus]

So he works and he builds with his own two hands
And he pours all he has in a castle made with sand
But the wind and the rain are comin' crashing in
Time will tell just how long his kingdom stands
His kingdom stands

He used to say, "Whoever dies with the most toys wins"
But if he loses his soul, what has he gained in the end
I'll take a shack on the rock
Over a castle in the sand

Now he works all day and cries alone at night
It's not getting any better
Looks like he's running out of time
[Chorus]

'Cause he worked and he built with his own two hands
And he poured all he had in a castle made with sand
But the wind and the rain are coming crashing in
Time will tell just how long his kingdom stands
His kingdom stands

All they really wanted was you
All they really wanted was you
All they really wanted was you

Comprehension

1 Retell the story of Jack's "career" in your own words.

Analysis

2 Analyze the structure of the song (stanzas, chorus, rhythm, rhymes, etc.).
3 Read Matthew 7: 24-27 and analyze the importance of the Biblical image of "building one's house on sand" in the song.

Opinion

4 Can religion provide a working alternative to chasing a materialistic dream? Explain your position.

Project

5 Write a dialogue in which Jack tries to justify his behavior to his wife and child.
6 Write a diary entry in which Jack's son expresses his reaction to the fact that his Daddy cannot come to his game.
7 Use Info Sheet 14, collect other pop songs about the American Dream, and devise a Powerpoint presentation.

21 Some Relevant Statistics

It is no accident that James Truslow Adams coined the term 'the American Dream' when many Americans were suffering from the harsh realities of the Great Depression. The following statistics show that, about eighty years later, there still exists a deep gulf between the promise of the 'Dream' and the reality in which many dreamers find themselves.

Number of People below Poverty Line, 2008*

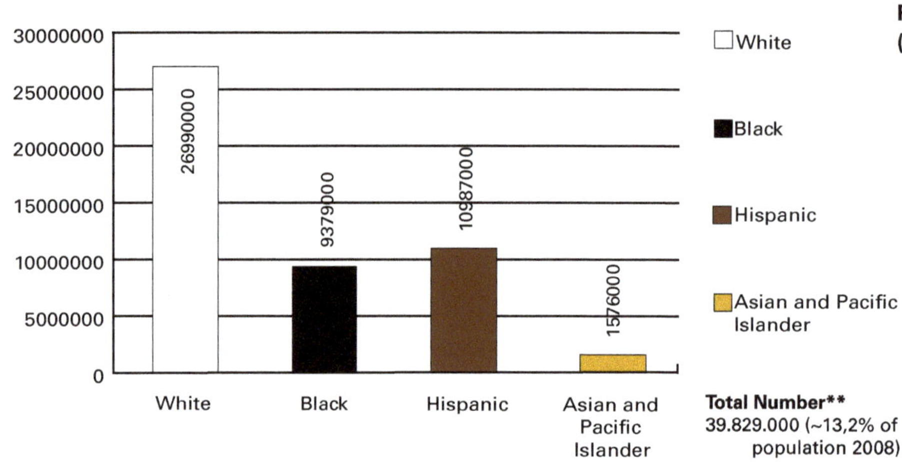

Total Number**
39.829.000 (~13,2% of population 2008)

Race of Death Row Inmates (Total: 3261)

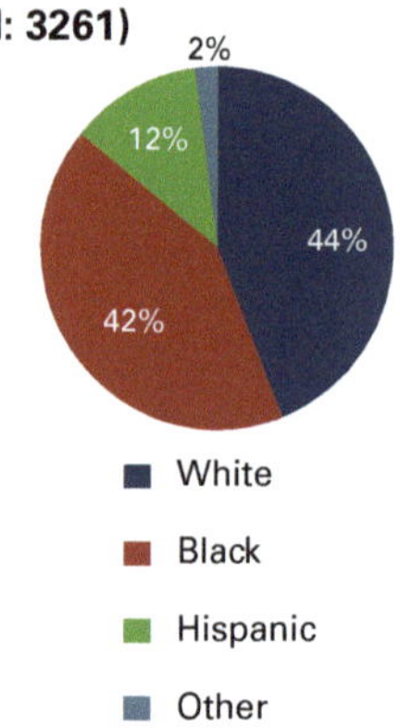

* For the official definition of Poverty, see Info Sheet

** Some respondents of mixed ethnicity were counted more than once

NATIONAL POPULATION: 308,745,538 United States Census Bureau

NATIONAL POPULATION BY RACE UNITED STATES: 2010

PERCENT OF POPULATION		CHANGE 2000-2010
White alone	72,4%	5,7% ↑
Black or African American alone	12,6%	12,3% ↑
American Indian and Alaska Native alone	0,9%	18,4% ↑
Asian alone	4,8%	43,3% ↑
Native Hawaiian and Other Pacific Islander alone	0,2%	35,4% ↑
Some Other Race alone	6,2%	24,4% ↑
Two or More Races	2,9%	32,0% ↑

NATIONAL POPULATION BY HISPANIC OR LATINO ORIGIN UNITED STATES: 2010

PERCENT OF POPULATION		CHANGE 2000-2010
Hispanic or Latino	16,3%	43,0% ↑
Not Hispanic or Latino	83,7%	4,9% ↑

Life Expectancy in Years

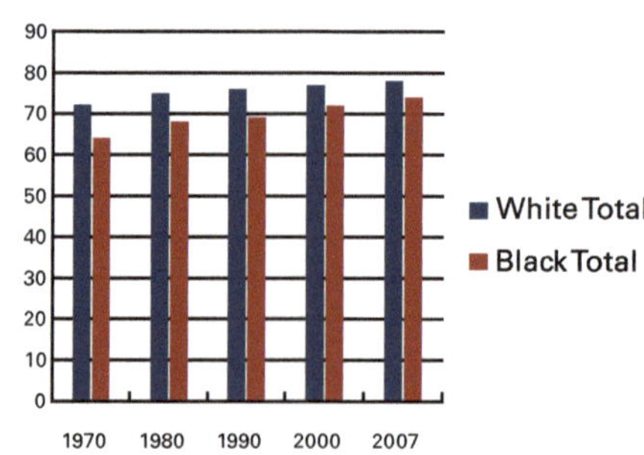

"The most formidable of all the ills that threaten the future of the Union arises from the presence of a black population upon its territory."
"The danger of a conflict between the white and the black inhabitants perpetually haunts the imagination of the Americans, like a painful dream."
Alexis de Tocqueville, *Democracy in America (1838)*

"Our nation is moving toward two societies, one black, one white, separate and unequal."
The National Advisory Commission on Civil Disorders (1968)

Competence Training

You can use this Viewfinder volume to practice most or all of the skills you will need to satisfy the requirements set out in the European Frame of Reference (up to level C1) and tested in exams like the German *Abitur* (all *Bundesländer*), TOEFL or IELTS. Details about all the skills (often referred to in German as *Kompetenzen*) that you can work to improve and which of the texts and/or sections from the book will be most useful in doing it are set out on these pages. They provide cross-references to the Viewfinder Reference Library (where you can find out exactly how to do things). You will get the RL from your teacher or you can download it from http://www.klett-sprachen.de. At the end there is a revi-sion checklist to make sure you can remember the main points the book deals with. This can be used for exam revision.

Language skills

Basic and advanced language skills
- grammar/structure
- vocabulary (new words, word formation)
- idiom
- register

Oral skills
- pronunciation
- intonation
- presentation

Written skills
- spelling
- punctuation
- text layout

All the texts in this book can help you practice and extend your competence in the active language skills of **speaking** and **writing** and the receptive skills of **reading** and **listening**. You should have learnt the basic language skills in English before you started working with this book. If you're not very confident yet, don't worry. You'll be able to practice all these skills and bring them up to a more advanced level working with any of the texts here. Some of the tasks are better for oral skills and others for written skills. Try to learn new words in their contexts (without trying to find the equivalent in your own language), and note down points which give you trouble, concentrating on learning them and checking your work specially to make sure you don't make the same mistake again. You will find a lot of helpful material in the Reference Library.

Speaking
- ability to pronounce English correctly (using correct accent and intonation)
- ability to use different idioms and registers
- managing discourse (making an appropriate choice of vocabulary, sentence structure, rhetorical devices, text structure) in, for example, everyday conversation or presentations

Listening
- comprehension of content
- ability to understand a variety of spoken text types (unscripted conversations, discussions; scripted news broadcasts, talks, speeches)
- being aware of rhetorical devices used by speakers
- ability to understand different social and geographical accents and dialects

Reading
- comprehension of content
- understanding of a writer's train of thought
- ability to recognise and understand a variety of text types, fictional and non-fictional

Writing
- ability to spell and punctuate correctly
- ability to write a number of different text types (essay, letter, report, presentation, commentary, analysis) using the appropriate vocabulary, grammar and text structure.

Don't forget: mistakes can be useful because you can learn from them, but repeated mistakes are a waste of time. The more proficient your English is, the more fun it will be to use, and the better impression it will make on your communication partners.

Text types

This volume contains the following types of non-fictional and fictional texts which you will be asked to analyse:

non-fictional texts	
interview	texts 3, 14
expository text/ monograph (excerpt)	introduction, texts 1, 9, 15
speech	texts 2, 4, 10, 14; background reading texts 4, 9
essay / article	texts 12, 16, 17, 18, 19; background reading texts 4, 9
letter	text 8
journal entry	introduction
astronomical diary	background reading text 8
autobiography / biographical interview	texts 12 (time table), 14

fictional texts	
novel (excerpt)	text 13; background reading to texts 3
poem	texts 5, 6, 7
lyrics	text 20

visual texts	
chart, graph, and diagram	texts 6, 17, 21
photograph	introduction, texts 1 (questions 1, 8), 4, 5, 10, 16, 18
cartoon	introduction (3, 4); texts 2 (11), 13 (5, 6), 15 (4), 17 (1, 2)
portrait	texts 2, 4, 5, 6, 10, 12, 14
painting	introduction (2, 6); texts 7 (7), 8 (3-5), 9, 11, 12 (8)
advertisement	texts 2 (3), 3, 8 (5), 16, 19
woodcut	text 6 (1)
poster	texts 2 (3), 14
magazine cover	text 3 (10)

Particular study skills when approaching texts

The tasks and questions which follow each text are designed to develop skills and competences in a number of areas: language practice and understanding, analyzing and appreciating a wide variety of fictional and non-fictional texts. The tasks will also enable you to develop your own ideas on the topics dealt with, and motivate you to carry out further research into areas that interest you.

Awareness:
Before reading a text you should be aware of certain ideas, facts, expectations or prejudices which form the context of the text itself. A skill to practice in all texts is:
note taking; this is a key skill for
a) preparing for discussions and
b) reading and analyzing texts (see below)

Other skills to practice here include:

Collecting and collating ideas:	
brainstorming (RL B 2)	introduction (question 1), texts 1(1), 4(1), 13(1),
making lists	introduction (3, 8), texts 1(3), 3(4), 6(3), 7(2), 10(4), 14(4), 17(5), 19(3)
question and answer session	texts 1(4), 2(2,5,7-9), 3(5), 4(2-4), 9(4-7), 10(1,2), 12(2-4), 13(2,4,5), 18(1,2,4), 19(1,2)
reports on individual experience	introduction (7), 3(7), 12(1,10)
general discussions	introduction (4), texts 1(7), 2(1,21), 4(8), 12(12,13), 14(6)

library research	texts 3(10), 4(9,11), 8(6)
internet research	introduction (8-10), texts 1(8), 2(18), 4(12,13), 5(4), 6(7), 14(6), 18(7)
film research (RL C2.2)	texts 4(11)

During reading you can practise a number of skills:

- skimming for general impressions
- scanning to find out facts or information
- note-making (RL A 4)
- marking important passages
- deducing meanings from context
- using a monolingual dictionary (RL A 3)
- using a bilingual dictionary (RL A 3)
- dividing the text
- summarising (RL C 3)
- finding the deeper meaning
- appreciating aesthetic qualities

In this *Viewfinder* you can practice all these skills on any text. Usually, apart from skimming, you will need to read a text at least three times. The questions under the heading 'Comprehension' are designed for the first seven skills on the list; the 'Analysis' questions will help you practice the last four skills.

After reading:

After you have read the text there are 'Analysis' and 'Opinion' questions to help you discover more meaning in the text, and think about what it means for you personally or what its implications are. You can do these questions alone, in pairs or groups, or as a class. You can answer them individually, present your answers to a plenum, or present them in writing.

Individual answers can be in the form of clearly organized notes or an essay.
Individual written answers can be in the form of a presentation based on notes.
Make sure your answers are clear and concise and relevant.
Check that your listeners have understood your answer.

Answers can also be produced orally or in writing in pair-work or group-work. This will enable you to practice the following teamwork skills:

- using the opportunity of practising English without being supervised
- organising and dividing up tasks
- co-operating and pooling ideas and skills
- using appropriate research tools
- practising time-management skills (keeping to a timetable)
- choosing an appropriate type of presentation
- using media as presentation aids.

The 'Opinion' questions can be used for various forms of discussion, argument or debate and to practice oral communication skills (see RL B 2). The following tasks are particularly suitable: introduction (questions 6,7), texts 1(7), 2(11,12,17), 3(7,8), 4(8), 5(3), 9(13), 10(4), 12(11), 14(5), 15(4), 16(4), 17(3), 18(6), 19(4), 20(3)

Textual analysis skills

The text analysis questions form the core of your coursework in the *Oberstufe*; their aim is to help you
a) work out what meanings the text might have for you and other readers
b) discover how the text affects you and the means used to achieve this
c) make judgments and write about the content of the text, its value, and its relevance to you.

NON-FICTIONAL TEXTS:

establishing types of text (RL C 1.2.1)	e.g. political speech: texts 2,4,10,14; interview: 3,14; letter: 8; argumentative essay: 16,17,18; statistics: 21;
content (fact v. opinion etc.) (RL C 1.2.1)	texts 1(questions 3-6), 2(11-13), 3 (4-7), 4(5,7,8), 8(1,2), 9(10-13), 10(3,4), 12(6,7), 14(5), 15(4,5), 16(2,4), 17(3), 18(1-4,6), 19(3,4)
structure and form (RL C 1.21)	texts 4(6), 9(3), 12(5)
function (RL C 1.2.2)	texts 2(1), 4(12)
style and tone (RL C 1.2.2)	texts 2(6,7), 4(6,7,10,12), 14(2)
recognizing humor and irony	background reading text 3(3); 17(1,2) and any cartoon
integrating visual components	texts 2 (3,11), 9(15),12(8),13(5),17(1,2)

FICTIONAL TEXTS:

genre (RL C 1.1)	novel excerpts: background reading text 3,13; poem: texts 5,6,7; lyrics: text 20
theme (RL C 1.1)	texts 5(1), 6(3,5), 7 (info box, 3), 13(2,4), 20(3); background reading text 3(3,6)
character and characterization (RL C 1.1)	texts 8(5), 13(2)
setting and atmosphere (RL C 1.1)	texts 5(4), 6(3,7), 7(2)
structure and formal aspects (RL C 1.1)	texts 5(2), 6(info box, 2), 9(5,6), 20(2)
style (RL C 1.1)	texts 5(2), 6(info box, 2)
tone (RL C.1)	texts 6(info box, 2)

Listening comprehension skills

Any of the texts can be used for listening comprehension if you listen to someone reading them, make notes and answer questions or summarise the text. In this context, speeches are particularly relevant because they are delivered publicly and the intonation will often imply the speaker's overall goal. Watching film scenes will also test listening comprehension skills. If the speaker is a non-native speaker of English, his pronunciation and intonation may differ from standard American English.

Texts that are particularly useful in this context are:	texts 2, 3, 4, 5(6), 10, 14
Texts and music	text 20

The CD contains several audio texts and videos which can also be used for listening comprehension.

Visual text comprehension skills

reading cartoons	introduction (questions 3,4), texts 2(3,11), 7(1,2), 12(9)
analysing photographs	texts 1(1,8), 5(4), 13(5,6)
analysing films	texts 4(11), 14(6)
comparing text and film	text 14 (6)
analysing paintings	introduction (2,6), texts 6(1), 7(7), 8(3-5), 9(15), 13
analysing charts, graphs, and diagrams	text 21

Particular writing skills / creative writing skills

that you can practice in 'Projects' or on the whole text:

essay	any text (esp. 10(7),18,19)
letter	any text (esp. 8,10,12,14,17)
e-mail	any text (esp. 17,10,14)
story	any text (esp. 3,13)
speech	any text (esp. 2,4,10,14,21)
petition	any text (esp. 17,18,19)
short descriptive text	texts 8(2), 10(3), 20(1)
newspaper article	texts 13(3)
dialogue	text 20 (3)
presentation	texts 4(13), 20(6)
report	text 3(10)

Intercultural Skills

Intercultural linguistic skills:
When you use another language you need intercultural skills. Languages differ fundamentally in the ways they express thoughts, or even sometimes in the thoughts they choose to express. So there is no such thing as word-for-word translation. Just think, e.g., of the differences between the German word *fahren* and the English *drive*. Or where you might write: "Mit diesem Bild will der Autor die Unmenschlichkeit des Krieges ausdrücken," in English we might say "The author uses this image to express the horrors of war."

So when working with this book you need to develop skills in relation to the use of the foreign language:

- **Intercultural linguistic** awareness: e.g. seeing how differently words and structures are used in English from their 'equivalents' in your language;
- **Intercultural linguistic competence:** e.g. being able to use the foreign language in the way that members of that language community use it;
- **Register and tone:** e.g. being able to recognize and use different registers like academic or colloquial, or different tones like serious, humorous or sarcastic.

All the texts in this volume expect you to work in the medium of English, which will help you to practice these skills. Specifically, you may be required to actively use various types of equivalents between English and your own language. This will involve the following skills:

- **Translation** (German: *Übersetzung*): Here you must find the nearest possible written equivalent in the other language while making sure that it reads like an original text in terms of structure, idiom, register and tone. This is particularly difficult in literary texts where you have to think of the aesthetic effect as well.
- **Interpreting** (German: *dolmetschen*): As an interpreter you must try to give the nearest equivalent possible of someone's spoken words, either after they have said them, or simultaneously.
- **Conveying the sense** (German: *Mediation*): People may want to know the sense, or message, of a document. They need to know the important facts and figures, but the particular linguistic expressions used in the original are irrelevant.

The texts (or extracts from them) in this *Viewfinder* volume most suitable for translating or conveying the sense are 1, 2, 9, 12, 14. You could also convey the sense of particular positions, like those of the speakers in texts 2, 3 or 13. For a real challenge you could try to translate 4, 6 or 7.

This *Viewfinder* volume *The American Dream* deals with a nation of immigrants in which different cultures interact, and so it is particularly useful for practicing intercultural skills. Although the different ethnic groups in the U.S. share the American Dream, they associate it with different hopes and aspirations and don't have the same chance of realizing it. Thus, the texts assembled in this *Viewfinder* topic teach students to be aware of similarities and differences within a multicultural society.

intercultural awareness	texts 1, 4, 5, 21
empathizing with others	texts 3, 4, 5, 21

socio-historical contexts	the concept of the Dream: texts 1, 2, 3; *translatio imperii* / the 'discovery' of America: texts 6-9; the notion of success / Social Darwinism: texts 12-14, 20
contemporary problems	introduction, race and poverty: texts 4, 5, 21; owning a house / the mortgage crisis: texts 15, 16; SUVs and the environment / a 'new' American Dream: texts 17-19

Particular tasks will give help in practicing these skills:

national unity and identity	texts 1, 2, 3, 4, 6–11; 12, 13, 14 (the notion of success), 17
religion	texts 4 (Martin Luther King), 6-11 (Manifest Destiny), 21
globalisation and ecology	texts 7-10; 16-19
poverty	texts 1, 2 (the Down Payment Fund), 3 (the Dream as a lottery), 4, 5, 12-14 (success); 15-16 (the mortgage crisis)
prejudices and stereotypes	texts 3, 4, 6 ('Indians'), 21 (crime and race)
integration and equality	texts 3, 4, 5, 21 (crime and race)
conflicts and reactions	texts 1, 4 (discrimination of blacks), 6-11 (conquest of the New World), 21 (inter-ethnic relationships)

Revision

As preparation for exams and assessments, it is a good idea to revise the main points you've learnt in this Viewfinder. The information may be useful if you are asked questions about this topic, or as background knowledge to put things into context. And if you are sure about these points it will boost your confidence.

Since the American Dream is a complicated and constantly changing concept, this Viewfinder can't offer an exhaustive treatment, but must concentrate on representative aspects.

The first section introduces the concept of the Dream, explores the coinage of the term by James Truslow Adams in the midst of the Great Depression, and investigates the use of the Dream notion for widely different political purposes in presidential speeches from Richard M. Nixon to Barack Obama. It also shows what 'average' American citizens think about the Dream and their chances of realizing it, and it illustrates the variety of ethnic dreams by presenting the doubts and hopes with regard to African Americans' "dream deferred" as expressed by Langston Hughes and Martin Luther King, Jr.

The second section deals with early European images of America and the role of the 'New World' in the history of *translatio imperii* as expressed in two influential poems by Michael Drayton and George Berkeley, and it investigates the crucial role of the West and the Frontier as understood by Josiah Strong, Senator Albert J. Beveridge, John Gast, Lyman Beecher, Horace Greeley, John L. O'Sullivan, and Frederick Jackson Turner. Thus, it traces the genesis of what the nineteenth century called 'manifest destiny' and what modern scholars define as American exceptionalism.

The third section explores the concept of personal success with regard to its religious roots as expressed by Benjamin Franklin and the influence of Social Darwinism as fictionalized by Theodore Dreiser, and it portrays Arnold Schwarzenegger as a contemporary example of the 'self-made man.'

The last section contrasts the promise of the Dream with a faulty reality by investigating the dream of owning a house and its abrupt end in the Subprime Mortgage Crisis and by providing some relevant statistics. It then illustrates both the opinion that the Dream is over as expressed by Paul Harris and Valdis Wish and the attempt to formulate a new, ecologically responsible and sustainable American Dream as propagated by The Sierra Club and the organization 'New American Dream' and as expressed in the Christian rock music of Casting Crowns.

On the following page you'll find a list of the major ingredients of the American Dream.

THE MAJOR INGREDIENTS OF THE AMERICAN DREAM

The belief in social PROGRESS
- the future-oriented belief in a steady improvement of individual, communal and societal conditions of existence
  - things will get continually better
  - the children will be better off than the parents

The belief in individual SUCCESS
- the conviction that everybody can realize their highest ambitions by means of their own endeavors
  - (in contrast to Europe) one needs no helpful connections
  - "from rags to riches" / "pull yourself up by your own shoestrings" / "vom Tellerwäscher zum Millionär"

The belief in American EXCEPTIONALISM or what the 19th century called MANIFEST DESTINY
- the certainty that God has singled out America as his chosen country and appointed the Americans to convert the rest of the world to true American-style democracy
  - export the American way of life to other countries
  - "make the world safe for democracy"

The belief in ever new FRONTIERS
- the assurance that, in the context of civilization's irresistible westward movement, ever new borderlines are to be crossed and obstacles to be surmounted
  - the 'open frontier' of the West (geographical; horizontal)
  - the 'open frontier of opportunity' (social; vertical)
  - the 'open frontier of space' (Kennedy)
  - the 'frontier of science' (nano-technology; cloning; etc.)

  ATTENTION: BE *frontier* /'frʌntɪə/ means 'the border of a country'; AE frontier /frʌn'tɪr/ means, in Turner's famous phrase, "the meeting point between civilization and savagery."

The belief in LIBERTY and EQUALITY
- the belief in the American form of government of the people, by the people and for the people
- "life, liberty, and the pursuit of happiness"
  - no class distinctions
  - everybody can participate

The belief in the MELTING POT or its recent mutation, the **MULTICULTURAL QUILT**
- the idea that immigrants of different nationalities, different ethnic stock, different religions and languages can be fused into a new nation
  - the 'melting pot' (a new breed as the result of the mixture of different ethnic groups)
  - the 'salad bowl' (initial differences remain visible)
  - the 'multicultural quilt' (peaceful togetherness without mixing)

  [discussed in greater detail in the Viewfinder topic From Melting Pot to Multiculturalism: E pluribus unum?]

The belief in additional concepts such as
  - the cult of NEWNESS
  - the glorification of YOUTH
  - the belief in unhampered MOBILITY
  - the belief in ever **NEW BEGINNINGS**

Contents of Reference Library